Complete Conditioning for
TENNIS

United States Tennis Association

Paul Roetert, PhD
Sport Science Administrator
United States Tennis Association

Todd S. Ellenbecker, PT, CSCS
Clinic Director
Physiotherapy Associates Scottsdale Sports Clinic

Human Kinetics

Library of Congress Cataloging-in-Publication Data

United States Tennis Association
   Complete conditioning for tennis / United States Tennis
Association.
      p.   cm.
   ISBN 0-88011-734-6 (pbk.)
   1. Tennis--Training.   2. Exercise.   I. Title.
GV1002.9.T7U55   1998
796.342--dc21   98-18354
                                                                  CIP
ISBN: 0-88011-734-6

Developmental Editor: Lynn M. Hooper-Davenport; **Managing Editor:** Coree Schutter; **Assistant Editors:** Jennifer Goldberg, Jennifer Miller, and Erin Sprague; **Copyeditor:** Denelle Eknes; **Proofreader:** Sarah Wiseman; **Graphic Designer:** Stuart Cartwright; **Graphic Artist:** Francine Hamerski; **Photo Editor:** Boyd La Foon; **Cover Designer:** Jack Davis; **Photographer (cover):** Russ Adams Productions, Inc.; **Photographer (interior):** Todd Ellenbecker, except where otherwise noted. Photos on pp. 48, 51, 56, 58, 72, 76, 77, 78, 79, 90, 93, 97, 191 by Vic Ramos; **Illustrators:** Joe Bellis and Jennifer Delmonte, Mac art; Beth Young, medical art; Keith Blomberg, line art; **Printer:** Versa Press

Human Kinetics books are available at special discounts for bulk purchase. Special editions or book excerpts can also be created to specification. For details, contact the Special Sales Manager at Human Kinetics.

Printed in the United States of America   10   9   8   7   6   5   4   3   2   1

Human Kinetics
Web site: http://www.humankinetics.com/

United States: Human Kinetics, P.O. Box 5076, Champaign, IL 61825-5076
1-800-747-4457
e-mail: humank@hkusa.com

Canada: Human Kinetics, 475 Devonshire Road Unit 100, Windsor, ON N8Y 2L5
1-800-465-7301 (in Canada only)
e-mail: humank@hkcanada.com

Europe: Human Kinetics, P.O. Box IW14, Leeds LS16 6TR, United Kingdom
(44) 1132 781708
e-mail: humank@hkeurope.com

Australia: Human Kinetics, 57A Price Avenue, Lower Mitcham, South Australia
(088) 277-1555
e-mail: humank@australia.com

New Zealand: Human Kinetics, P.O.Box 105-231, Auckland 1
(09) 523-3462
e-mail: humank@hknewz.com

CONTENTS

FOREWORD

Today's tennis players are bigger, faster, and stronger than ever before. Modern racket technology allows players to hit the ball at speeds never thought imaginable—serves on the men's tour are traveling at speeds over 140 miles per hour. The physical demands facing tennis players have never been more challenging.

Participating in tennis was much simpler in the 1950s and 60s when my twin brother, Tim, and I were growing up in Onalaska, Wisconsin. We played the sport when it was in season—as we did football, basketball, and baseball—and we didn't follow a specific or elaborate training program. We ran a few laps, we did some sprints, and we did a few sit-ups and push-ups. That was a pretty typical approach to tennis conditioning back then.

That all changed in the 1980s, as Ivan Lendl and Martina Navratilova demonstrated the benefits of tennis-specific training. Ivan and Martina took advantage of the knowledge gained through the sport sciences to enhance their mental skills, biomechanics, nutrition, aerobic conditioning, and strength and flexibility training. Both players enjoyed long and lucrative pro careers, and won several Grand Slam titles, because they were dedicated to becoming the best athletes they could be through hard work and a commitment to conditioning.

The tougher the match and tournament, the more important conditioning becomes. As captain of the USA Davis Cup team, I have witnessed many outstanding performances in difficult conditions before less-than-friendly foreign crowds. Because every match in Davis Cup is the best of five sets, fitness is always a key factor. And as Olympic coach for the 1996 U.S. Men's Tennis team, I saw our athletes face the challenge of keeping focused amidst a wide array of terrific sporting events.

The conditioning programs, workout routines, and exercises in *Complete Conditioning for Tennis* provide players a proven tennis-specific training plan to improve their fitness and their game. The book will benefit players of all ages and ability levels, and is a great resource for coaches and tennis teaching professionals. The USTA's advice on training and injury prevention is the best information available in the world in our sport.

I hope this book helps improve your health, fitness level, and ultimately your tennis game.

Tom Gullikson
Davis Cup Captain
Olympic Coach
USA Tennis Director of Coaching

PREFACE

As the lob sailed over her partner's head, she yelled, "Switch," and ran back to cover the shot. A point from the U.S. Open Tennis Championships? No, rather a typical point played at the U.S. Tennis Association's National 65-and-Over Championships. These players already know what many others are just finding out: tennis may be the perfect sport, not only to help you live longer but also to improve the quality of your life.

Much of a person's fitness decline is caused by disuse and not by aging, according to Dr. Robert Leach, a member of the USTA Sport Science Committee and an avid tennis player. Leach has observed that people who started playing tennis at a young age and continued throughout their lifetimes retained a very high level of fitness. And even if you haven't played in a long time, you can still get significant benefits by resuming the sport in later life. Tennis is a great sport because you can get quality exercise with built-in rest periods, and you can have fun competing at every age and level.

So, we know that playing tennis will improve your fitness level. However, we also know that a high fitness level will improve your tennis. Of course by playing often and taking lessons you will progress, but proper, tennis-specific conditioning may be the most important factor in improving your game. That is the reason for this book. We offer you guidance in designing your own training program, no matter what level player you are. The material in this book is based not only on scientifically sound information, but also on our experience working with top players, experienced coaches, and expert conditioning specialists.

THE MODERN GAME

Bill Tilden, in his 1925 book, *Match Play and the Spin of the Ball*, stated, "There are two general rules of body position so elemental in tennis that

I should omit them from this book, but to make this chapter complete, I must restate them.

1. Await a stroke facing the net, with body parallel to it.
2. Play every stroke with right angles (sideways) to the net. This is true for service, drive, chop, volley, smash, half-volley and lob."

Bill Tilden would be amazed if he could see the techniques that modern players use. Certainly, he could not have foreseen the open stance forehands, the two-handed backhand, and the speed of the game. Turning sideways to the net on every stroke is more time consuming, and it also allows less power generation. Of course racket technology has a lot to do with it. Rackets are longer, racket heads are bigger, frames are wider, sweet spots are larger, and rackets are made of stiffer materials. It seems that whatever material was used on the space shuttle is now used to make tennis rackets. Materials like boron, kevlar, titanium, and graphite have replaced the wood rackets Bill Tilden played with. All this has added to the speed of the game, as well as changes in technique. To deal with these changes, prevent injuries, and perform at the highest levels, players must condition themselves properly.

TRAINING TECHNIQUES

An average point, even on a clay court, probably won't last more than 10 seconds. During this time, you may have as many as four or five direction changes. Following a point you will have a 25-second rest period and on the changeovers a 90-second rest period. This clearly makes tennis an anaerobic sport, requiring agility and speed. However, a tennis match can last as long as three hours. Therefore, aerobic conditioning and muscular endurance come into play as well. Having a good aerobic base will help you recover between points, and muscular endurance will improve muscle strength and may correct muscle imbalances from the one-sidedness of tennis. Reaching for wide shots and jumping for overheads requires power as well as flexibility. Clearly, to be a good tennis player you need a properly designed, tennis-specific training program. This book provides the tools and information to make your own *Complete Conditioning for Tennis* program.

ACKNOWLEDGMENTS

We would first and foremost like to thank Ron Woods of the USTA for encouraging us to go ahead with this project and providing us with valuable feedback along the way. Rainer Martens and Ted Miller, as always, were great to work with and came up with the original idea for this series. Lynn Hooper-Davenport and Coree Schutter were a big help with the organization and editing process.

This book would not have happened without the conditioning information we have been exposed to along the way. Experts like Michael Bergeron, Greg Brittenham, Jeff Chandler, Don Chu, George Davies, Mark Grabow, Jack Groppel, Bill Kraemer, Jim Loehr, Mike Nishihara, Janet Sobel, and Ron Witchey, along with members of the USTA Sport Science committee, have helped us design many of the drills and exercises and were always willing to share their knowledge with us. Of course, we should also mention the national coaching staff, in particular Tom Gullikson, Lynne Rolley, Nick Saviano, and Stan Smith for their interest in sport science and for always letting us share our latest conditioning techniques with the players.

Last, but not least, we wish to thank USTA sport science staff members Barrett Bugg and Laura Selby for reviewing this manuscript and helping with the revisions.

Key to Diagrams

P   Players

C   Coach or partner

T   Target

     Cone

⟶   Path of Player

— — —   Ball feed from Coach

○   Ball

CHAPTER 1

PHYSICAL DEMANDS OF TENNIS

Todd Martin and Michael Chang

are top-ranked tennis players and have won many titles. However, Todd is 6 feet 5 inches and Michael, 5 feet 7 inches. This is one great advantage tennis has over other sports. Players with different heights and body structures can be successful. Todd uses his big serve and looks for any opportunity to use his large wingspan at the net, and Michael plays a baseline game, running down most every shot. One thing they have in common is their excellent training habits and physical fitness level. In this book we will look at what it takes, besides stroke technique, to become a good tennis player. Players now look for any advantage, and having a well-designed training program is critical in reaching the top. This book will cover all aspects of complete conditioning for tennis.

FITNESS DEMANDS OF A TENNIS MATCH

Researchers characterize tennis as a sport in which players must respond to a continuous series of emergencies. Sprinting to the ball, changing directions, reaching, stretching, lunging, stopping, and starting. All these characteristics, combined with maintaining proper balance and technique throughout a match, are critical for optimal performance on the court. Therefore, players must address flexibility, strength and endurance, power, agility and speed, body composition, and aerobic and anaerobic fitness to improve their tennis games. What follows is a brief overview of the components of fitness for tennis players. Each component will be explained more fully in later chapters.

© Russ Adams Productions, Inc.

Flexibility

Tennis requires you to make shots that place your body parts in extreme ranges of motion (e.g., when your arm is fully extended over your head reaching for a lob). Throughout a match you are called on to generate great force from a variety of body positions; changing direction, reaching for a shot, stopping quickly, and serving are a few examples. Strength throughout a flexible, unrestricted range of motion will help prevent injury and enhance performance.

Strength and Endurance

Have you ever played in a long match that made your muscles sore the next day? Well, that's because tennis requires you to have not only good strokes, but also excellent strength and muscular endurance. Throughout a match, you may hit hundreds of balls while running from side to side. Good muscular endurance, which means that you can apply force and sustain it over time, can help you hit the ball just as hard at the end of a match as at the beginning. Also, it can help prevent injuries.

Power

Tennis requires explosive movements. Greater power allows you to respond more quickly and produce forceful movements with less effort. Players with explosive first steps get into position quickly, set up well, and hit effective shots. In addition, an explosive first step will give you the speed to get to balls hit farther away. Both upper and lower body power are necessary in tennis. To maximize your power, you must transfer your lower body power to the upper body.

Agility and Speed

Agility is crucial to good court movement. It allows you to be in the correct position and provides a solid platform from which to hit the ball. In a typical five-second point, there may be as many as four direction changes. Speed is important to get to the ball. Though some people have natural speed, others can achieve this by training their muscles and nervous systems to produce the same effect. The faster you can get to a ball, the more time you have to prepare for your shot.

Optimum Body Composition

The amount of bone and water your body consists of remains constant, so you should pay attention to muscle and fat when attempting to alter body composition. You can increase the amount of muscle in the body through proper strength training. However, it is not enough to increase muscle mass; you also must maintain an appropriate level of body fat. The two ways to affect body fat are fat-loss dieting and aerobic exercise. Fat-loss dieting, which is the correct term for a weightloss diet because you are attempting to decrease fat in particular, is a method of decreasing fat intake while maintaining an adequate caloric intake. Along with using fat as an energy source, aerobic exercise will improve your endurance in longer matches. Body fat percentages to shoot for are approximately 8 to 18 percent for men and 15 to 25 percent for women. By following a balanced diet and including aerobic exercise (a few sets of tennis) in your training regimen, these percentages will be attainable.

© Russ Adams Productions, Inc.

Anaerobic and Aerobic Fitness

What's the best way to train for tennis? To answer that question, let's look at the energy demands of the sport. The energy used in a long-distance race comes from the aerobic (with oxygen) system, and the energy used in short bursts of activity, such as a 20-yard dash, is called anaerobic (without oxygen). Although it is difficult to quantify the energy demands of tennis, we know that it is a sport that relies on strong aerobic and anaerobic systems.

Most points in tennis, even on a clay court, last less than 10 seconds, whereas the average point on a hard court between two equally matched players lasts approximately 5 seconds. A player may expend 300 to 500 short bursts of effort during a match. Each short burst of effort is an anaerobic activity. So, obviously anaerobic training is important.

Does that mean you can ignore aerobic training? No! In a tennis match you have 25 seconds of rest between points and 90 seconds between games. If your aerobic fitness is low, it is difficult to recover between points and games, and you are likely to get tired at the end of a match. Another advantage of a strong aerobic base is that it provides you with the endurance to have quality workouts. Therefore, because matches

© Russ Adams Productions, Inc.

can last a long time and players must recover quickly between points, aerobic fitness is key as well.

All these components of physical fitness are important in developing your game. To help you create an appropriate program that enhances your performance, reduces injury risk, and increases your lifetime enjoyment in the game, start by designing a proper periodization training program (chapter 9 includes examples of these training programs).

PLANNING YOUR CONDITIONING PROGRAM

To obtain the best results in reaching your optimal fitness level, start by learning the demands of a tennis match. Then, by designing a periodization training program, set realistic performance goals. Tailor periodization training programs to your individual needs, and modify them as your fitness level, tournament schedule, or goals change. Each concept and activity we cover in the following chapters should fit into your periodization program. Decide which tournaments for the upcoming year are most important to you. Then, determine your baseline fitness level by testing yourself using the USTA Fitness Testing Protocol (see chapter 2). Once you've identified the areas you need to focus on, use the exercises, workouts, and sample training schedules in chapters 3 through 9 to design a customized training program for yourself. The information in chapter 10 will help you prevent training injuries.

TESTING TENNIS FITNESS

What makes Pete Sampras and

Steffi Graf such great tennis players? Their skill level is obviously outstanding. They hit great serves, ground strokes, and volleys. However, they not only hit the ball well, but also work hard on their physical fitness. No matter what your ability, you can't play your best tennis if you're not physically fit. Being physically fit means that your heart, blood vessels, lungs, and muscles can function at maximum efficiency. When you are fit, your body adjusts more easily to increased physical demands.

FITNESS TESTS FOR TENNIS

The USTA has determined the essential components of fitness and designed a fitness testing protocol based on these components. The components are flexibility, strength and endurance, power, agility and speed, body composition, and aerobic capacity.

Keeping track of your fitness testing results can help you pinpoint strengths and weaknesses, design or refine a training program, and monitor your progress. From the test results, you and your coach can determine which fitness areas you need to improve. You can then design a specific training program based on your results. Using the test results of many junior tennis players, the USTA has established fitness ranges for different age groups and genders. Properly interpreting your results can help you determine the relative position of a fitness score in the distribution, recognizing weak areas for injury prevention and performance enhancement.

You can create your profile detailing your score relative to other players your age and gender. The sample player in figure 2.1 is a right-handed male player in the 18-and-under division. His results clearly indicate high scores in the strength and power categories. However, his scores in the speed and agility areas were significantly lower than other players in his age group. This player should concentrate on improving his movement skills on the court, using drills in chapters 6 and 7. Fitness testing every few months should indicate your improvement in the different categories. It will also show you where you need to modify your training program. Now let's look at each fitness component.

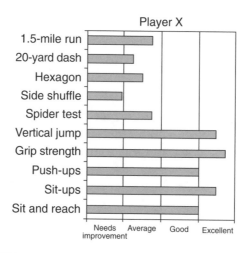

Figure 2.1 Sample player profile.

Compare Your Scores

The ranges listed in the charts after each fitness test are guidelines based on normative data collected by testing junior and adult tennis players. Junior player norms are based on data collected from nationally and regionally ranked 18-and-under junior players, as well as collegiate players and young touring professionals. Adult player norms are based on data collected from avid tennis players aged 25 and over.

FLEXIBILITY TESTS

Flexibility is the motion available (how far you can move around) at a joint (e.g., shoulder, elbow, wrist, hip, knee, ankle). If a muscle cannot stretch, allowing the joint to move through a full range of motion, both injury risk and performance may be affected. The shoulder and low back are the most frequently injured body parts in elite tennis players. Players such as Mary Joe Fernandez have found that a regular stretching routine can lengthen a career significantly.

Performance on the court depends mostly on your tennis skill. However, being inflexible may prevent you from moving efficiently, affecting the proper execution of your strokes. Are you able to touch your toes while keeping your knees straight? If not, you are like many tennis players who have poor low-back or hamstring flexibility. The hamstrings include three muscles at the back of the thigh. Because they attach to the lower pelvis, they create tension in the low back. Good flexibility in the hamstrings will improve torso flexibility and should decrease incidence of low-back injuries. The sit-and-reach and hamstring flexibility tests will indicate how much work you need in this area.

Several research studies have indicated a relationship between the loss of shoulder internal rotation flexibility and the number of years a player has competed. This loss of shoulder flexibility appears to get worse with longer periods of play. Early detection by testing your shoulder flexibility can help improve performance and reduce the risk of injury.

Sit and Reach

On the men's professional tennis tour, 38 percent of players have missed at least one tournament because of low-back problems. Hitting tennis balls not only involves extending the body, but also requires a lot of twisting. The key to having good flexibility is to stretch your muscles regularly (see chapter 3). This will help you, not only in preventing injuries but also in reaching the wide shots that you could never get to before. How do you know if you are flexible enough? Take a sit-and-reach test and see if you can reach past your toes. This test measures the flexibility of the lower back and hamstrings.

Procedures

1. Sit with your knees extended and legs flat on the floor. Have a partner hold your knees so they do not come off the floor.

2. Lean forward with your arms extended and have your partner measure the distance from your fingertips to your toes. Your hands should be next to each other.

3. Record your score. If you do not reach your toes, the number is recorded negatively in inches. If you do reach past your toes, the number is recorded positively in inches.

4. Compare your scores with those in table 2.1.

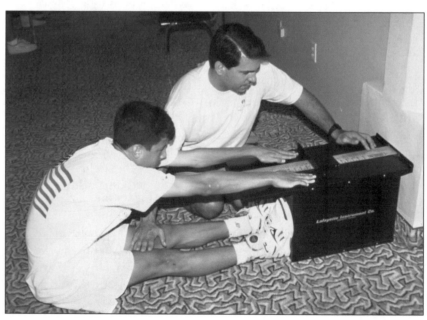

© 1998 Allese and Morton Pechter

Sit and reach test.

Table 2.1   Sit and Reach (inches)

Female	Excellent	Good	Average	Needs Improvement
Adult	>6	4-6	2-4	<2
Junior	>8	7-8	5-7	<5

Male	Excellent	Good	Average	Needs Improvement
Adult	>3	1-3	0-1	<0
Junior	>4	2-4	1-2	<1

Hamstring Flexibility

Hamstring flexibility measures the amount of stretch in the muscle at the back of the thigh. Tennis players use this muscle for stopping, starting, running, and jumping. In your next practice, after you have warmed up, try a lunge (one leg reaches forward as the back leg stays stationary) as if you were reaching for a wide volley. If you feel tightness in the back of your thigh, your flexibility is probably not enough to make this shot without potential injury. If not properly stretched, this muscle can be easily strained or injured by the fast movements in tennis.

Procedures *(This test should be administered by a trained professional.)*

1. Lie down on a table with a partner stabilizing your pelvis (holding down your hip bone).
2. Raise one leg until you feel tightness in the back of the leg.
3. Your partner measures the angle at the hip with a goniometer.
4. Repeat on the other side.
5. Compare your scores with those in table 2.2.

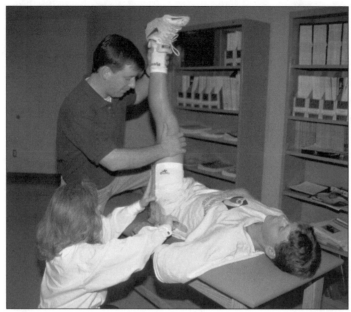

© Lance Jeffrey

Hamstring flexibility test.

Table 2.2   Hamstring Flexibility (degrees)

	Excellent	Good	Needs Improvement
Female	>85	85-75	<75
Male	>80	70-80	<70

Shoulder Flexibility

Shoulder flexibility describes how far you can move your arm around your shoulder joint. Adequate range of motion, both internally and externally, is essential for injury prevention and good technique during the strokes. With your upper arm at a 90-degree angle to your upper body (abduction), internal rotation is when your fingers point toward your toes. External rotation is when your fingers point above your head. If the internal or external rotator muscles are tighter than they should be, imbalances and shoulder injuries are likely to occur. Many tennis players have poor internal rotation flexibility.

Procedures *(This test should be administered by a trained professional.)*

1. Lie down on a table with a partner stabilizing your scapula (holding down your shoulder blade).
2. Your upper arm is at a 90-degree angle to the upper body (abduction). The elbow is also bent at a 90-degree angle (pointing at the ceiling). This is considered the neutral position.
3. Rotate your arm internally and externally and have your partner measure both angles of rotation with a goniometer.
4. Repeat on the other side.
5. Compare your scores with those in table 2.3.

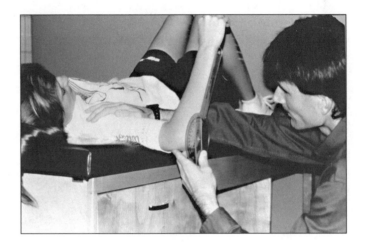

Shoulder flexibility test.

Table 2.3   Shoulder Flexibility (degrees)

Female	Dominant	Nondominant
External	95-105	95-105
Internal	45-55	55-65

Male	Dominant	Nondominant
External	95-105	90-100
Internal	40-50	50-60

MUSCLE STRENGTH AND ENDURANCE TESTS

Strength is the amount of weight you can lift or handle at any time. Muscular endurance is the number of times your muscles can lift a weight or how long your muscles can hold a weight.

A recent study of collegiate tennis players showed that a nine-month program of strength training improved the velocity of the players' serves, forehands, and backhands by as much as 35 percent. In addition, the players lowered their body fat and increased their lean muscle mass. These players found out what many top professionals already know: improving your strength and endurance can add years to your playing career and help you hit the ball harder in the process.

The abdominal muscles contract almost every time you hit the ball forcefully. In addition, with more players hitting open-stance forehands, additional stress is put on the musculature of the abdominal wall due to an increase in upper body rotation. Sit-ups develop those muscles that are responsible for flexing or bending the trunk in a forward motion and protecting them from injury while hitting your strokes.

Strength in the upper body is imperative not only to hit the ball harder, but also to prevent injuries to the shoulder, elbow, and wrist. Push-ups will indicate overall shoulder, chest, and triceps strength, and the grip-strength measurement can show not only forearm strength, but also differences between the dominant and nondominant side.

Sit-Ups

We all know that it is important to have strong legs to help you get around the court as fast as possible and that you need a strong arm to provide a forceful swing. Equally important may be your abdominal and low-back muscles. These muscles serve as an important link between the lower and upper body as you transfer force from the ground all the way up to the racket. They contract at a high intensity while executing most tennis strokes. For training purposes, you may want to perform crunches to reduce the strain on your hip flexors and low back (see pages 76-77 for crunches). However, for testing purposes, we always recommend that someone hold your feet while you perform a complete sit-up. Sit-ups test your abdominal strength and endurance.

Procedures (*Players with a history of low-back pain should not perform the following test.*)

1. Lie down on your back with your hips flexed at 45 degrees and knees flexed at 90 degrees.

2. Have a partner hold your feet so they don't move while you perform the sit-ups.

3. Cross your arms over your chest and place your hands on opposite shoulders.

4. Perform as many sit-ups as possible in a 60-second period (have your partner count and keep an eye on the clock).

5. To count as a complete sit-up, the elbows must touch the knees in the up position (while keeping the arms against the body), and the shoulder blades must touch the mat in the down position (hips must stay in contact with the mat).

6. Compare your scores with those in table 2.4.

Table 2.4 Sit-Ups (number completed in 1 minute)

Female	Excellent	Good	Average	Needs Improvement
Adult	>53	46-53	42-46	<42
Junior	>54	46-54	35-46	<35

Male	Excellent	Good	Average	Needs Improvement
Adult	>58	51-58	47-51	<47
Junior	>63	56-63	50-56	<50

Push-Ups

So you want to hit your serve as hard as Sampras. Performing push-ups may not guarantee that you'll be able to serve 130 miles an hour; however, having strong shoulders and arms can help you hit the ball harder and reduce your risk of injury. If doing a full push-up is too hard, start by doing wall push-ups, then progress to modified push-ups (from the knees). This should prepare your upper body for those big serves you're planning to hit. Push-ups test your upper body strength and endurance.

Procedures

1. Get in a prone position with hands shoulder-width and the weight of your lower body on your toes.

2. Extend your arms, but keep your head, shoulders, back, hips, knees, and feet in a straight line.

3. Have a partner record the number of push-ups you complete in a 60-second period or to failure.

4. To count as a complete push-up, the upper arm must reach parallel to the floor or below in the down position, the arms must be completely extended in the up position, and you must maintain a straight body alignment.

5. Compare your scores with those in table 2.5.

Table 2.5 Push-Ups (number completed in 1 minute)

Female	Excellent	Good	Average	Needs Improvement
Adult	>44	34-44	27-36	<24
Junior	>42	34-42	20-34	<20

Male	Excellent	Good	Average	Needs Improvement
Adult	>49	40-49	30-40	<30
Junior	>52	49-52	35-49	<35

Grip Strength

Having good grip strength can help you prevent wrist and elbow injuries. In addition, it can help you hold on to your racket better on those off-center hits. Although your dominant arm will be stronger than your nondominant arm, professionals recommend that the difference between the two should not be greater than 25 percent. Grip strength measures the strength of the finger flexors and forearm muscles.

Procedures

1. Hold your arm down at your side and squeeze a grip strength dynamometer (Available at a physical therapy clinic or university physical education or exercise physiology department.).
2. Record the result in kilograms (1 kilogram is 2.2 pounds).
3. Repeat on the other side.
4. Compare your scores with those in table 2.6.

Table 2.6   Grip Strength (kilograms)

Female	Excellent		Good		Average		Needs Improvement	
	Dom.	Non-Dom.	Dom.	Non-Dom.	Dom.	Non-Dom.	Dom.	Non-Dom.
Adult	>39	>27	34-39	24-27	28-34	22-24	<28	<22
Junior	>37	>33	34-37	27-33	31-34	25-27	<31	<25

Male	Excellent		Good		Average		Needs Improvement	
	Dom.	Non-Dom.	Dom.	Non-Dom.	Dom.	Non-Dom.	Dom.	Non-Dom.
Adult	>60	>36	51-60	31-36	42-51	26-31	<42	<26
Junior	>52	>42	48-52	34-42	39-48	31-34	<39	<31

POWER TESTS

Power is the amount of work you can perform in a given period. Power is needed during activities using both strength and speed. Improving either or both of these fitness components can help your athleticism tremendously. Picture Venus Williams or Pete Sampras in one of their well known "jump overheads." They have worked hard on improving the power in their games. Lower body power is important to get to the ball as rapidly as possible; upper body power helps you hit the ball hard throughout a match.

Both vertical jump and medicine ball testing are important to assess how powerful you are. The vertical jump measurement focuses on the lower body. Good scores on this test may indicate a quick and explosive first step in getting to the ball, as well as strong jumping ability on those tough to reach lobs. The medicine ball test involves the whole body and is more tennis specific. It may be interesting to compare your forehand and backhand scores, then to relate those scores to your forehand and backhand strokes to see if those strengths and weaknesses are similar. During the overhead tosses you should use the legs to obtain maximum distance.

Vertical Jump

Everybody is born with a certain amount of athletic ability; however, you can improve your vertical jump and lower body power. Training the lower body means developing an explosive first step. During an average five-second point in a tennis match, there can be as many as four direction changes. Therefore, it is important to develop powerful legs. The vertical jump is a measure of lower body power. It is the height you can jump from a standing position minus the height you can reach when standing.

Procedures

1. Stand with your side to a wall and touch it with your arm extended as high as possible.
2. Have a partner mark the spot.
3. Extend and attach a yardstick up the wall from the highest reach of your fingertips.
4. Put chalk on your fingers before you jump.
5. Jump with your side facing the wall (do not take a step), reaching as high as you can on the yardstick.
6. The difference between your standing reach and the highest point of your jump is your score.
7. Compare your scores with those in table 2.7.

Table 2.7   Vertical Jump (inches)

Female	Excellent	Good	Average	Needs Improvement
Adult	>21	16-21	12-16	<12
Junior	>22	17-22	13-17	<13

Male	Excellent	Good	Average	Needs Improvement
Adult	>27	22-27	17-22	<17
Junior	>28	26-28	21-26	<21

Medicine Ball Toss

Training with a medicine ball can be practical because you can mimic the tennis strokes. Tossing the medicine ball involves the whole body. There is a strong relationship between performing well in these tests and overall fitness in tennis players. Pay particular attention to the technique of the tosses. Proper technique will involve knee flexion and extension and a significant amount of trunk rotation, not a toss with the arms only. The medicine ball toss is a measure of power.

Procedures

1. Stand at a designated spot facing forward and hold a six-pound medicine ball.

2. Take one step and toss the ball, simulating a forehand stroke, while staying behind the line.

3. Measure the distance from the line to the point the ball landed.

4. Repeat for the backhand side.

5. Compare your scores with those in tables 2.8 and 2.9.

The overhead and reverse overhead tosses use the same muscle groups as the serve and overhead. You will be most successful if you use ground reaction forces properly. From physics we know that for every action there is an equal and opposite reaction. Releasing the medicine ball at a 45-degree angle will give you the best results. Both overhead and reverse overhead tosses are measures of power.

Table 2.8   Forehand Medicine Ball Toss (feet)

Female	Excellent	Good	Average	Needs Improvement
Adult	>30.5	25-30.5	19.5-25	<19.5
Junior	>32	26-32	20-26	<20

Male	Excellent	Good	Average	Needs Improvement
Adult	>39	32-39	25-32	<25
Junior	>42	35-42	28-35	<28

Table 2.9   Backhand Medicine Ball Toss (feet)

Female	Excellent	Good	Average	Needs Improvement
Adult	>30	24-30	17.5-23.5	<17.5
Junior	>31	25-31	18-25	<18

Male	Excellent	Good	Average	Needs Improvement
Adult	>37.5	30.5-37.5	23.5-30.5	<23.5
Junior	>42	34-42	26-34	<26

Procedures (Overhead)

1. Stand behind a line facing forward and hold a six-pound medicine ball.
2. Toss the ball as far as possible from an overhead position, using only one step. Do not cross the line.
3. Measure the distance from the line to the point the ball landed.
4. Compare your scores with those in table 2.10.

Procedures (Reverse Overhead)

1. Stand with your back facing the net and toss a six-pound medicine ball backward.
2. Using an underhanded position, toss the ball as far as possible.
3. Measure the distance from the net to the point the ball landed.
4. Compare your scores with those in table 2.11.

© Lance Jeffrey

Starting position for overhead toss.

Table 2.10   Overhead Medicine Ball Toss (feet)

Female	Excellent	Good	Average	Needs Improvement
Adult	>22.5	18.5-22.5	14.5-18.5	<14.5
Junior	>23	19-23	15-19	<15

Male	Excellent	Good	Average	Needs Improvement
Adult	>30.5	25.5-30.5	20-26.5	<20
Junior	>34	29-34	23-29	<23

Table 2.11 Reverse Medicine Ball Toss (feet)

Female	Excellent	Good	Average	Needs Improvement
Adult	>32.5	26.5-32.5	20.5-26.5	<20.5
Junior	>34	27-34	20-27	<20

Male	Excellent	Good	Average	Needs Improvement
Adult	>43.5	35-43.5	27-35	<27
Junior	>46	38-46	31-38	<31

AGILITY AND SPEED TESTS

Agility and speed are your ability to move around the court quickly and smoothly to position yourself for a shot. Agility is crucial to good court movement. It allows you to be in the correct position and provides a solid platform from which to hit the ball. Speed is important to get to the ball.

In a study of elite junior tennis players, researchers found that agility was the most important physical fitness component in predicting a player's ranking. We know that speed in tennis does not entail running long distances. When you see Venus Williams and Michael Chang sprinting around the court, they usually only have to run a few yards before changing directions. They seem to do this effortlessly and with balance. Determining how quickly you move while keeping control of your balance could be the first (explosive) step to reaching that ball you could never reach before.

Playing tennis requires you to move in every possible direction. Although the 20-yard dash indicates your straight ahead speed, which you may sometimes need when you are on the dead run for a drop shot, the sideways shuffle shows you your lateral speed or how fast you can move from side to side. The spider run combines these movements in a tennis-specific way. The movement pattern involves sprinting as well as changes in direction. The hexagon drill will force you to control your upper body so your center of gravity will stay close to your base of support when conducting this test.

Hexagon

The hexagon test measures foot quickness in changing direction backward, forward, and sideways while facing in one direction (facing in the same direction during the test simulates facing your opponent during a match). The hexagon test also tests your ability to stabilize the body quickly between those direction changes, because you need stability before you can perform the next jump. If the body is not stabilized, you will lose your balance.

Procedures

1. On the ground, use masking tape to create a hexagon (six sides with angles of 120 degrees). Make each side 24 inches long.

2. Stand in the middle of the hexagon and remain facing in the same direction throughout the test.

3. When your partner gives you the command, "ready, go," jump forward over the tape and immediately back into the hexagon (your partner should be timing you with a stopwatch).

4. Continuing to face forward, jump over the next side and back to the middle. Repeat for each side.

Hexagon test.

5. Continue this pattern by jumping over all six sides and back to the middle each time for three full revolutions of the hexagon.

6. When the feet enter the hexagon after three full revolutions, your partner should stop the clock and record your time.

7. Give yourself one practice trial.

8. Test yourself twice, recording both times with the stopwatch, then note your best time.

9. Compare your scores with those in table 2.12.

Table 2.12   Hexagon (seconds)

Female	Excellent	Good	Average	Needs Improvement
Adult	<12.00	12.00-12.10	12.10-12.40	>13.40
Junior	<10.48	10.48-11.70	11.70-12.30	>12.30

Male	Excellent	Good	Average	Needs Improvement
Adult	<11.80	11.80-13.00	13.00-13.50	>13.50
Junior	<11.10	11.10-11.80	11.80-12.70	>12.70

Twenty-Yard Dash

Michael Chang and Arantxa Sanchez Vicario are two of the fastest players in professional tennis. It's no wonder they're also at the top of the rankings. You can't hit a good shot if you don't have enough time to get in position. An average point in tennis lasts between 5 and 10 seconds. Therefore, explosive speed is important. Training short-distance sprints taxes the anaerobic system (see chapter 5). The 20-yard dash measures speed.

Procedures

1. Mark off 20 yards on a tennis court with masking tape (the distance from the baseline to the opposite side service line is exactly 20 yards).

2. Have a partner stand at the finish line with arm in the air and stopwatch in hand.

3. At the drop of the arm and the command, "ready, go," sprint toward the finish line.

4. Record your score.

5. Compare your scores with those in table 2.13.

Table 2.13 20-Yard Dash (seconds)

Female	Excellent	Good	Average	Needs Improvement
Adult	<3.30	3.33-3.40	3.40-3.60	>3.80
Junior	<3.20	3.20-3.36	3.20-3.54	>3.62

Male	Excellent	Good	Average	Needs Improvement
Adult	<3.20	3.20-3.30	3.30-3.50	>3.50
Junior	<2.90	2.90-3.00	3.00-3.30	>3.30

Spider Run

Remember the old shuttle run in school? Well, the spider run is tennis' version of the shuttle run. Of all the physical fitness tests we administer to players, the movement patterns in this test most closely simulate the movements during a tennis match. The stopping and starting actions of this activity make it an excellent test as well as a great training drill. The spider run tests your speed and agility.

Procedures

1. Using masking tape, mark off a 12-by-18-inch rectangle behind the center of the baseline, using the baseline as one side.

2. Position five balls on the court: one on each corner where the baseline and singles sideline meet, one on each side where the singles sideline and service line meet, and one ball on the T.

3. Have a partner record your score with a stopwatch.

4. Start with one foot in the rectangle; retrieve each ball and place it in the rectangle, one at a time in a counterclockwise direction.

5. As soon as you place the last ball in the rectangle, your partner stops the time.

6. Compare your scores with those in table 2.14.

Table 2.14   Spider Run (seconds)

Female	Excellent	Good	Average	Needs Improvement
Adult	<17.30	17.30-18.00	18.00-18.30	>18.30
Junior	<17.10	17.10-17.16	17.16-17.34	>17.34

Male	Excellent	Good	Average	Needs Improvement
Adult	<15.00	15.00-15.30	15.30-16.00	>16.00
Junior	<14.60	14.60-15.00	15.00-15.40	>15.40

Sideways Shuffle

Many speed and agility tests measure your forward speed; however, just as important in tennis is lateral speed. You spend much of your time on the baseline shuffling from side to side, retrieving forehands and backhands. Moving quickly while staying balanced (keeping your center of gravity over your base of support) is critical in this exercise. The sideways shuffle is a speed and agility test focusing on lateral movement.

Procedures

1. Start on the center service line at the T, with one foot on either side of the line, facing the net.

2. Have a partner record your score with a stopwatch.

3. While facing the net, shuffle along the service line, touch the doubles sideline, then shuffle to the opposite doubles sideline, and continue back to the center. Crossover steps are not allowed.

4. Compare your scores with those in table 2.15.

Table 2.15   Sideways Shuffle (seconds)

Female	Excellent	Good	Average	Needs Improvement
Adult	<6.0	6.0-7.0	7.0-7.3	>7.3
Junior	<7.0	7.0-7.1	7.1-7.4	>7.4

Male	Excellent	Good	Average	Needs Improvement
Adult	<6.4	6.4-6.7	6.7-7.0	>7.0
Junior	<5.5	5.5-5.6	5.6-5.7	>5.7

BODY COMPOSITION TEST

Knowing your *body composition* is the result of measuring, through various methods, the percentages of fat, muscle, bone, and water that your body is made of. Percent body fat gives a good indication of your physical condition. Percentages to shoot for are listed in table 2.16. Of course you want to note that having too little body fat can be detrimental not only to your tennis game, but to your overall health, as well.

Body composition can be measured in a variety of ways. The skin fold method has been accurate and more cost effective than other methods. Because it takes practice to properly conduct skin fold testing, this test is usually administered by a trained professional, such as a physical therapist or exercise science specialist.

Skin fold measurements provide a simple and noninvasive method of estimating percent body fat. The sum of three sites is taken and entered into an equation to predict body composition.

Procedures (*This test should be administered by a trained professional.*)

1. The sites measured for men are chest, abdomen, and thigh. The sites measured for women are triceps, suprailium, and thigh.

2. Add the three skin fold measurements together. Then use a formula available from a trained professional to calculate the percentage of body fat.

3. Compare the percentage to those listed in table 2.16.

Body composition test: Skin fold measurement.

Table 2.16   Body Composition (suggested ranges for tennis players)

	Female	Male
Adult	15-25%	8-20%
Junior	12-22%	5-15%

AEROBIC ENDURANCE TEST

Aerobic endurance is the ability to take in, transport, and use oxygen. Aerobic energy is used during prolonged, steady-paced activities, mainly using the large muscle groups. Examples include jogging, cycling, and swimming.

Aerobic endurance is important in tennis. When you become more aerobically fit, you can recover faster between points and perform longer before getting tired. As your endurance improves, your ligaments and tendons will become tougher, reducing the threat of injury and laying the foundation for more intense training.

We all know you need a lot of endurance to play on the slow clay of Roland Garros during the French Open Championships. Players like Sergi Bruguera and Thomas Muster can battle for hours on the red dirt. However, keep in mind that even if you don't have access to a clay court, hard-court tennis also requires stamina. A strong aerobic base will allow you to recover efficiently between points, even throughout long, close matches. To see if you're in good enough shape for those tough matches, test your aerobic fitness.

One accurate and simple test to measure your aerobic fitness is the one and one-half mile run. If you do it on a track, you can easily test a single player or a group of players. Because this is a common test, you can also make comparisons with available data from other sports.

Although tennis involves many short sprints on the court, there is also an aerobic component. Matches can last three hours or longer, taxing the aerobic system. When completing the one and one-half mile distance, you should focus on running at a consistent pace throughout all six laps. You should train for longer distances in the off-season and preseason.

Procedures

1. Stand at the start-finish line on a level 440-yard track (we recommend cinder or tartan tracks).

2. A partner gives the command, "ready, go" and starts the stopwatch.

3. Complete one and one-half miles (six laps) and record your score.

4. Compare your scores with those in table 2.17.

Table 2.17   1.5-Mile Run (minutes:seconds)

Female	Excellent	Good	Average	Needs Improvement
Adult	<11:49	11:49-13:43	13:43-15:08	>15:08
Junior	<10:30	10:30-11:00	11:00-11:30	>11:30

Male	Excellent	Good	Average	Needs Improvement
Adult	<8:44	8:44-10:47	10:47-12:20	>12:20
Junior	<9:45	9:45-10:15	10:15-11:00	>11:00

TENNIS FITNESS PACKAGE

Many factors contribute to success in tennis, and because tennis is a skill sport, just being strong or fast does not make you a better player than someone else. However, you can always improve your physical abilities and address your weaknesses. Top players are constantly looking for an edge over their opponents. They can all hit the ball well, so proper fitness training may be that difference in putting them ahead of the competition. Why wouldn't you test yourself on these fitness components just like the pros do? Keeping track of fitness testing results can help you track your performance, reduce the risk of injury, and develop a better understanding of your fitness abilities. You can then design proper training programs as outlined in chapters 8 and 9, based on your individual needs.

CHAPTER 3

WARM-UP AND FLEXIBILITY

In a recent interview, John McEnroe

was quoted as saying "Stretching allows me not to get injured and to move around a little quicker." McEnroe, one of America's greatest champions, was plagued during his career with hamstring, groin, and low-back injuries. He now appreciates the benefits of stretching, and in that same interview said, "As I've gotten older, my hamstrings have gotten really tight, so that's something that I really stretch." Regardless of their age, tennis players can benefit from stretching before and after they play and train.

A quality conditioning program for tennis includes strength, flexibility, and endurance, as well as anaerobic and aerobic training. If any component in tennis players' training programs is neglected, players are unlikely to achieve their full performance potential and are more susceptible to injury while playing. Tennis demands proper warm-up and flexibility training for all areas of the body. Injuries to the upper and lower extremities as well as the trunk have been reported in elite and recreational players and will be discussed in chapter 10.

WARMING UP

The warm-up plays an important part in the tennis player's conditioning program. You should perform warm-up exercises before working on flexibility as shown in table 3.1. The purposes of the warm-up are to prepare the body tissues to optimally respond to the exercises and stretches applied during the workout and to prevent injury. Athletes often use two types of warm-up. A passive warm-up involves applying an external heat to the body. Examples of passive warm-up methods include applying moist heat packs, heating pads, or a warm whirlpool before exercise. These techniques increase tissue temperature, but are not always practical. A second type of warm-up is the active warm-up and involves low-intensity exercise, which elevates tissue temperature, increases heart rate, and actively prepares the athlete for exercise.

Recommended Activities

- Jumping jacks
- Calisthenics
- Slow jogging or jogging in place
- Low-intensity stationary cycling
- Large arm circles (clockwise and counterclockwise)

Working until you experience a light sweat indicates the proper duration and intensity of a warm-up. Using the recommended activities, you can often achieve this in three to five minutes. Additional benefits of a proper warm-up are improved tissue elasticity and a reduced risk of muscle and tendon injury.

Table 3.1   Incorporating Stretching Into Tennis

---

1. General body warm-up (three to five minutes) to increase tissue temperature (slow jog, jumping jacks, etc.).
2. Static stretching of tight and restricted areas.
3. Dynamic stretching with progressive increases in range and velocity of movements.
4. Playing tennis.
5. Static stretching cool-down to prevent muscle soreness and gain flexibility.

FLEXIBILITY TRAINING

Flexibility training is often the most overlooked and least adhered to component of a quality conditioning program. Some reasons for this include

- stretching doesn't feel good;
- flexibility's benefits on the court are not obvious to the player;
- most players have no specific, individualized guidelines for how, why, what, and when to stretch; and
- flexibility receives less emphasis by coaches than the other components of conditioning.

We define *flexibility* as the degree to which the muscles, tendons, and connective tissue around the joints can elongate and bend. Performing nearly all tennis strokes requires the tissues to elongate and bend. There are several types of flexibility. Static flexibility describes the amount of motion you have around a joint or series of joints while at rest. Dynamic flexibility refers to the active motion about a joint or series of joints and represents the amount of movement the player has available for executing serves, ground strokes, and volleys. Dynamic flexibility is limited by the resistance to motion of the joint structures (bones and ligaments); the ability of the soft connective tissues to deform (muscles and tendons); and neuromuscular components of the body, which include the nerves.

Factors influencing flexibility include heredity, neuromuscular components, and tissue temperature. Regarding heredity, body design determines our overall flexibility potential. Although most people tend to be inflexible, some are loose jointed or hyperflexible. Aspects of heredity and body design that affect our flexibility potential include the shape and orientation of joint surfaces, as well as the construction and design of the joint capsule, muscles, tendons, and ligaments.

A second factor influencing flexibility involves neuromuscular components. The muscle spindle is a watchdog mechanism, located between the muscle fibers. When you stretch a muscle too quickly, the muscle spindle sends a message to the central nervous system (CNS) to contract the muscle. With this stretch reflex, the muscle shortens and contracts, hindering the stretching process. Therefore, when stretching, we recommend a slow, gradual movement to minimize the reflex action of the muscle spindle and enhance the stretching process.

The third factor influencing flexibility is tissue temperature. Heat increases the elongation and bending properties of soft tissue. Warming up before stretching by raising the body's core temperature or by breaking a light sweat will give you greater gains in flexibility, with less microtrauma to the tissues you are stretching. Later in this chapter we will discuss how to incorporate stretching into a tennis training program.

AREAS NEEDING FLEXIBILITY TRAINING

Few people are as flexible around their joints as they need to be, and tennis places tremendous demands on different body parts in their extremes of motion. For example, the range of motion the shoulder needs during the external rotation of the serve greatly stresses the front of the shoulder. Tennis players are flexible in this external shoulder rotation due to the service motion, but exhibit limited internal rotation on their tennis playing side.

To demonstrate this, try to touch your hands behind your back as pictured in figure 3.1a by placing your racket arm behind your head and neck and nonracket arm behind your back. Many players can touch or nearly touch their hands together in this position. Now reverse the positions of your hands, and try to touch your hands together as the right-handed player is doing in figure 3.1b. You can clearly feel that it is more difficult to touch your hands when your racket arm is coming up from behind your back.

This demonstrates the increased flexibility of external rotation on the racket arm, as well as decreased flexibility of internal rotation. To address this flexibility imbalance, we recommend specific stretches for the muscles in the back of the shoulder (external rotators). We do not recommend exercises that stress the front of the shoulder by placing the arms behind the body (such as in a doorway) for tennis players and throwing athletes.

Additional examples of extreme ranges of motion during tennis play include

1. lateral movement patterns that stress the hip and groin,
2. stabilizing muscle actions of the abdominal muscles during the tennis serve, and
3. explosive movement patterns by the calf muscles and Achilles tendon.

Throughout a match, players must generate great force and speed while in an outstretched position. A conditioning program that includes flexibility exercises ensures that you will have the range of motion you

a   b

Figure 3.1   This right-handed player exhibits normal internal rotation in her nonracket arm (a) but limited rotation in her serving arm (b).

need for optimal performance. Flexibility, combined with the ability to produce power in these extremes of motion, is essential in tennis. Stretching alone *will not* prevent injury or enhance performance; however, balanced strength throughout a flexible, less restricted range of motion will. You can only attain this goal by using a complete conditioning program for tennis.

Benefits of Flexibility

- Allows sport-specific strengthening in motion extremes
- Accommodates the stresses by helping tissue distribute impact shock and force loads more effectively
- Lightens the work of opposing muscle groups by providing less restricted motion
- Enhances blood supply and tissue nourishment
- Allows good form without compensation from other body segments
- Overcomes imbalances created by the sport and by daily activities

FLEXIBILITY EXERCISES

One of several types of flexibility exercises, ballistic stretching involves quick bounces at the motion extremes. Because it is potentially harmful and offers no significant benefits over other techniques, we *do not* recommend ballistic stretching. Ballistic stretching often elicits the stretch reflex, so it can hinder flexibility by starting a self-protective mechanism in a muscle, causing it to shorten. Ballistic stretching can cause injuries because of the danger of going beyond the tissue's elongation and bending limits.

A second, highly recommended type of flexibility exercise is static stretching. Static stretching involves slow, isolated, smooth movements and passively holding the extreme range. It is the most practical and effective method and can improve flexibility safely and effectively. Done correctly, it requires minimal energy and creates little danger and no soreness. Table 3.2 lists the procedures we recommend for static stretching.

A third type of flexibility exercise is dynamic stretching, which simulates the movements in the sport without the stresses of weight bearing or impact. This type of stretching is effective just before playing. The body part actively goes through the tennis motions with control. The motion is gradually exaggerated, increasing the size of the flowing motions. Table 3.3 lists examples of dynamic stretches.

Table 3.2 Static Stretching

---

1. Warm-up three to five minutes.

2. Emphasize slow, smooth movements and coordinate deep breathing. Inhale deeply, exhale as you stretch to the point of motion just short of pain, then ease back slightly. Hold this static stretch position for 15 to 20 seconds as you breathe normally. Repeat two or three times.

3. You should not feel pain. If it hurts, or if you feel a burning, you are stretching too far.

4. Stretch your tight side first.

5. Stretch only to your limits.

6. Do not lock your joints.

7. Do not bounce.

8. Stretch larger muscle groups first, and repeat the same routine each day.

9. An ideal time to stretch is just after aerobic activity.

Recognizing the critical role of flexibility in peak performance and injury prevention, the United States Tennis Association Sport Science committee has put together recommendations for a flexibility-training program. Flexibility needs are specific to each individual and joint.

You can use tests that measure flexibility to identify areas of inflexibility and to demonstrate progress in a specific flexibility program. An example of an appropriate test for flexibility is the sit-and-reach test, which measures low-back and hamstring flexibility (see page 9 in chapter 2).

You can assess combined shoulder internal rotation by placing the back surface of both hands with the thumbs pointing up in the low back, reaching up toward the shoulder blades as high as possible. Although the dominant arm is not likely to reach as high as the nondominant arm in tennis players (see figure 3.1a and b), the stretches for the back of the shoulder should enhance this range of motion and decrease the difference between the two shoulders. A more specific way of measuring shoulder internal and external rotation is with a goniometer (see page 11 in chapter 2). A physical therapist, athletic trainer, or exercise physiologist can properly measure shoulder internal and external rotation and perform other tests to measure flexibility.

Figure 3.2, a-b depicts the human muscular system for reference when designing your flexibility program. In many instances in this chapter we include more than one flexibility exercise for each body part because some exercises are more basic than others. If one area of the body has limited range of motion, you may want more than one stretching exercise for that body segment. Once you can perform one stretch, you may

---

Table 3.3   Dynamic Stretching

---

1. Swing the racquet in each motion arc—forehands, backhands, and serving motions.

2. Reach up with alternating arms, as if climbing a ladder, incorporating your trunk into each movement.

3. With hands on your hips, bend to each side.

4. With hands on the ends of the racquet held overhead, bend side to side.

5. Holding the racquet with your hands on the ends, rotate your trunk by twisting side to side.

6. Make a bicycle motion with each leg, drawing progressively larger circles.

7. March, alternating legs, until your knee is up at nose height.

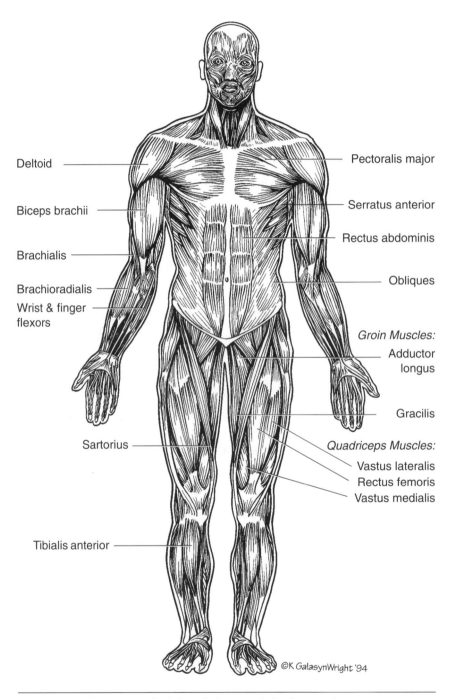

Deltoid

Biceps brachii

Brachialis

Brachioradialis

Wrist & finger flexors

Pectoralis major

Serratus anterior

Rectus abdominis

Obliques

Groin Muscles:
Adductor longus

Gracilis

Sartorius

Quadriceps Muscles:
Vastus lateralis
Rectus femoris
Vastus medialis

Tibialis anterior

©K GalasynWright '94

Figure 3.2a Front view of adult male human skeletal musculature.
©K. Galasyn-Wright, Champaign, IL, 1994.

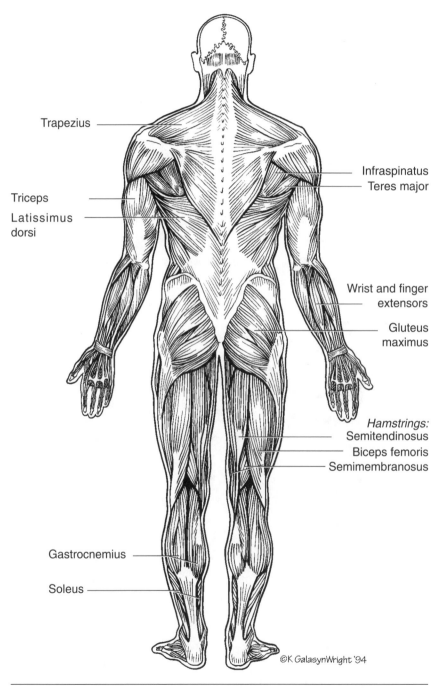

Trapezius

Infraspinatus
Teres major

Triceps

Latissimus
dorsi

Wrist and finger
extensors

Gluteus
maximus

Hamstrings:
Semitendinosus
Biceps femoris
Semimembranosus

Gastrocnemius

Soleus

©K Galasyn Wright '94

Figure 3.2b   Rear view of adult male human skeletal musculature.
©K. Galasyn-Wright, Champaign, IL, 1994.

want a more advanced stretch for that area. We recommend focusing on areas of the body that are the most inflexible. We do not recommend stretching only areas that are the most flexible or easiest for the athlete to stretch. This will take time from other areas that need special attention and may decrease joint stability or promote imbalances.

SHOULDER AND ARM STRETCHES

TRUNK AND SHOULDER STRETCH

Focus: Latissimus dorsi, triceps, inferior capsule of the shoulder.

Starting Position: Stand with your arms overhead, holding the right elbow with the left hand.

Exercise Action: Use your left hand to pull the right elbow behind your head. Hold your elbow in this position, and bend your trunk to the left side. Repeat on the opposite side.

OVERHEAD STRETCH

Focus: Intercostal muscles, inferior capsule of the shoulder.

Starting Position: Stand with your arms overhead, wrists crossed, and palms together.

Exercise Action: Stretch your arms slightly backward and as high as you can. Bend a few inches to either side to increase the stretch to your trunk.

POSTERIOR SHOULDER STRETCH

Focus: Shoulder rotators, upper back (scapular) muscles.

Starting Position: Stand holding your right arm straight in front of you. Place your left hand behind your right elbow.

Exercise Action: Pull across your body with your left hand. *Do not* allow your trunk to rotate. It may help to stand against a wall and keep both shoulder blades touching the wall while performing the stretch.

SHOULDER SQUEEZE

Focus: Front of chest, back, shoulders.

Starting Position: With your fingers interlaced behind your head, keep your elbows straight out to your side and your upper body in an upright, aligned position.

Exercise Action: Pull your elbows together behind you, and pull your shoulder blades together to create tension through your upper back and shoulder blades.

FOREARM FLEXOR STRETCH

Focus: Forearm muscles (flexors and pronators).

Starting Position: The elbow is straight and the forearm is supinated (palm up).

Exercise Action: Use the opposite hand to stretch the wrist back (extension), keeping the elbow straight.

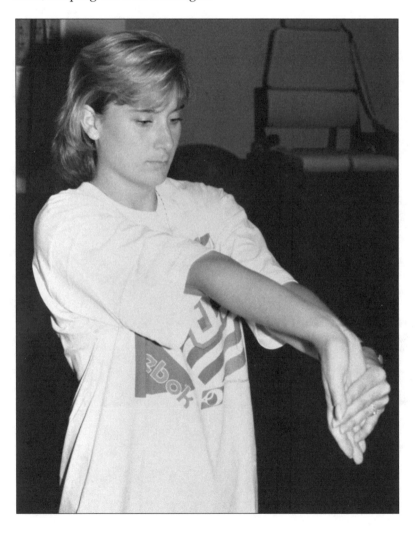

FOREARM EXTENSOR STRETCH

Focus: Forearm muscles (extensors and supinators).

Starting Position: The elbow is straight and the forearm is pronated (palm down).

Exercise Action: Use the opposite hand to stretch the wrist downward (flexion), keeping the elbow straight.

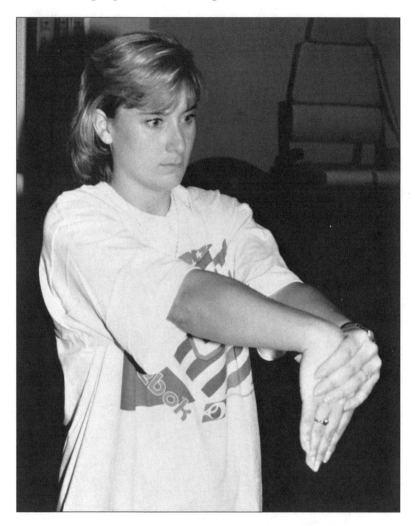

HIP AND LEG STRETCHES

FIGURE 4 HAMSTRING STRETCH

Focus: Hamstrings.

Starting Position: Sit with the leg you will stretch out in front, with the knee straight and toes pointing up. Bend the opposite knee and place the bottom of your foot against the extended knee.

Exercise Action: Keeping the back erect and the knee as straight as possible, reach forward with both hands toward your foot.

HAMSTRING STRETCH

Focus: Hamstrings, gluteals.

Starting Position: Lying on your back, bend the leg you will stretch to a 90-degree angle at your hip. Support the leg by grasping both hands behind the knee. Keep the opposite leg straight.

Exercise Action: Straighten the leg and raise it toward the trunk. Use the hands to gently increase the stretch. Point the toes toward the face to increase the stretch.

HAMSTRING SUPER STRETCH

Focus: Hamstrings, calf muscles.

Starting Position: Place the leg approximately waist high on an object (table or chair seat).

Exercise Action: Slowly bend forward at the waist, bringing your trunk toward your thigh. Bending the toes toward your face intensifies the stretch.

STORK QUADRICEPS STRETCH

Focus: Quadriceps, hip flexors.

Starting Position: Stand on one leg, bending the opposite knee while grasping the foot or ankle.

Exercise Action: Keeping the back flat and the buttocks tucked under, bend the knee, bringing the foot toward the buttock, and point the knee toward the ground. Do not twist the knee.

PRONE QUADRICEPS STRETCH

Focus: Quadriceps, hip flexors.

Starting Position: Lie on your stomach.

Exercise Action: Bend the knee toward the buttock while grasping the foot or ankle with your hand. Pull the foot directly toward the buttock; do not twist the knee.

GROIN STRETCH

Focus: Groin, inner thigh muscles.

Starting Position: In a standing position with your feet shoulder-width apart, place your hands on your hips.

Exercise Action: With the toes pointing slightly outward, slowly bend the knee until you feel a stretch in the groin area. Roll your weight onto the inside of the opposite foot.

SEATED GROIN STRETCH

Focus: Groin, inner thigh muscles.

Starting Position: Sit with the bottoms of your feet together, knees out, holding your toes.

Exercise Action: Gently pull forward, bending from the hips and bringing the chest to the feet. Do not round your upper back. Use your elbows to gently push the knees toward the ground.

HIP TWIST

Focus: Lateral hip muscles, low back.

Starting Position: Lie on your back with your knees bent, feet flat on the floor. Place your arms out to the side on the ground to stabilize the upper back. Place your left ankle outside the right knee.

Exercise Action: Use your left leg to pull your right leg toward the floor until you feel a stretch along the outside of your hip or lower back. Keep your upper back and shoulders flat against the floor. Do not touch the floor with the right knee, but stretch it within your limits.

PIRIFORMIS STRETCH

Focus: Piriformis muscle.

Starting Position: Lie on your back with the left knee bent. Place the right ankle just above the left knee.

Exercise Action: Slowly bring the left knee toward the chest. You will feel the stretch in the right buttock.

HIP ROTATOR STRETCH

Focus: Hip rotators, lateral hip, thigh muscles.

Starting Position: Lie on your back with your arms out to the side and your legs straight.

Exercise Action: Lift the exercise leg to 90 degrees, then lower it across the other leg. Keep your trunk and both shoulders on the floor throughout the stretch.

ILIOTIBIAL BAND STRETCH

Focus: Iliotibial band.

Starting Position: Stand with the right hand on the wall, your right leg approximately three feet from the wall and the left leg crossed over the right.

Exercise Action: Gently push the right hip toward the wall. Increase the stretch by standing farther from the wall.

CALF STRETCHES

Focus: Calf muscles (gastrocnemius, soleus).

Starting Position: Stand in front of a wall or fence with one leg two or three feet behind the other and the toes pointing forward.

Exercise Action:

a. Keeping the back knee straight and your heel on the floor, bend the front knee and lean the trunk forward. Do not arch the back.
b. Repeat with the back knee slightly bent, keeping the heel on the ground.

TRUNK STRETCHES

KNEE TO CHEST FLEX

Focus: Low back, gluteals.

Starting Position: Stand with your feet shoulder-width apart.

Exercise Action: Bend one leg and grasp the lower leg just below the knee. Slowly pull the knee toward the chest.

DOUBLE KNEE TO CHEST FLEX

Focus: Low back, gluteals.

Starting Position: Lie on your back with your knees bent.

Exercise Action: Bring the knees toward your chest by grasping the lower legs just below the knees.

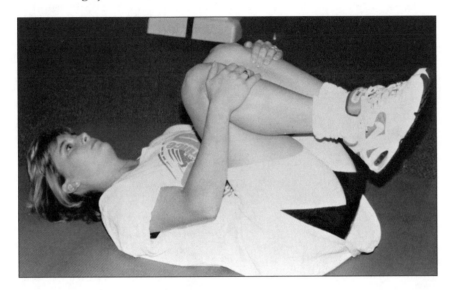

SPINAL TWIST

Focus: Low back, hip rotators.

Starting Position: In a seated position, place the right ankle outside the left knee.

Exercise Action: Bring the left arm around the right knee. Slowly turn the shoulders and trunk to the right, and look over the right shoulder.

CHAPTER 4

STRENGTH TRAINING

Players like Patrick Rafter and
Lindsay Davenport can hit the ball just as hard in the last game of the
final set as in the first game of a match. These professional players have
committed themselves to strength and power exercises that allow their
muscles to function at the highest level. This chapter will define common
terms, outline critical components of a strength-training program, and
give you examples of tennis-specific exercises to improve your muscular
strength and endurance.

We can define *strength training* as a type of exercise that requires the
body's musculature to move against an opposing force. *Strength* is the
maximum amount of force a muscle can produce. Tennis players must
have high levels of muscular strength, and, because of the repetitive
nature of the game, they must also be able to repeatedly contract their
muscles. *Muscular endurance* is the ability to repeatedly contract a muscle
or group of muscles.

© Russ Adams Productions, Inc.

Power is the amount of work per unit of time, and we can think of it as the explosiveness of the muscle or muscle group. Muscular power is a function of strength times speed. We can best illustrate how strength differs from power by comparing a bodybuilder with a tennis player.

A bodybuilder trains his or her muscles for up to six hours per day to achieve a desired muscular size, strength, and appearance. Training methods for the bodybuilder emphasize slow, forceful movements with heavy resistance levels, few repetitions, or low volume. Although body-builders can generate great force, they cannot generate power (force at high speeds) and lack the explosive movement abilities required for tennis. Training your muscular system for tennis requires lower resistance levels, more repetitions, and high-speed training exercises that allow the muscles to generate power. Training for tennis must address all three areas: strength, power, and endurance.

Table 4.1 shows which muscles are used during particular tennis strokes. We recommend targeting these frequently used muscles, as well as those muscles that stabilize and decelerate the body, with a tennis-specific, strength-training program that emphasizes concentric and eccentric actions.

Resistance Training Terms

Athletes use several forms of resistance training to develop muscular strength, power, and endurance. Tennis players use *isometric* strength training least often. Isometric strength training does not require the muscle fibers to shorten or lengthen and does not require joint movement. A common example of this static form of exercise involves placing the palms in front of the chest and pushing them against one another.

Another form of strength training is *isotonic*. Tennis players can use isotonic resistance training, which is more dynamic and uses a constant weight or tension (like a dumbbell or weight machine at a gym). This form of strength training involves joint movement and shortening and lengthening of the muscle fibers. There are two types of contractions that occur during isotonic strength training: concentric and eccentric.

In *concentric* contraction the muscle fibers contract and shorten. An example of concentric contraction is raising your hand and forearm toward your shoulder while doing a biceps curl. The elbow joint moves as the muscle fiber shortens. An *eccentric* contraction occurs when the muscle fiber lengthens. Using the biceps curl example, the eccentric contraction occurs as you slowly lower the hand and forearm away from your shoulder.

Table 4.1   Muscles Used in Tennis Drives, Volleys, and Serves

Muscles Used in the Forehand Drive and Volley

Action	Muscles Used
Push-off	Soleus, gastrocnemius, quadriceps, gluteals
Trunk rotation	Obliques, spinal erectors
Forehand swing	Anterior deltoid, pectorals, shoulder internal rotators, elbow flexors (biceps), serratus anterior

(continued)

Table 4.1 *(continued)*

Muscles Used in the One-Handed Backhand Drive and Volley

Action	Muscles Used
Push-off	Soleus, gastrocnemius, quadriceps, gluteals
Trunk rotation	Obliques, spinal erectors
Backhand swing	Rhomboids and middle trapezius, posterior deltoid, middle deltoid, shoulder external rotators, triceps, serratus anterior

Muscles Used in the Two-Handed Backhand Drive

Action	Muscles Used
Push-off	Soleus, gastrocnemius, quadriceps, gluteals
Trunk rotation	Obliques, spinal erectors
Backhand swing	
Nondominant side	Pectorals, anterior deltoid, shoulder interior rotators
Dominant side	Rhomboids and middle trapezius, posterior deltoid, middle deltoid, shoulder external rotators, triceps, serratus anterior

Muscles Used in the Serve and Overhead

Action	Muscles Used
Trunk rotation	Obliques, spinal erectors
Knee and hip extension before impact	Quadriceps, gluteals
Arm swing	Pectorals, shoulder interior rotators, latissimus, triceps
Arm extension	Triceps
Wrist flexion	Wrist flexors

Reprinted by permission, from USTA, 1993, *Strength Training for Tennis,* (White Plains, NY: USTA Player Development Publication Department), 18-19.

STRENGTH TRAINING FOR TENNIS

Tennis is a rapid, dynamic sport that requires powerful, repeated muscle contractions. Functional tennis conditioning must include dynamic strength training instead of static, isometric training.

The shortening and lengthening of the muscle fibers during training is important because tennis requires these muscle contractions in every stroke and body movement. Typically, players use eccentric contractions to decelerate and control or stabilize the body, and use concentric contractions to produce movement and accelerate the body. For example, eccentric contractions occur in your thigh muscle as you land on your leg and recover to hit a wide forehand or backhand ground stroke. Concentric contractions occur in the front of your shoulder as you accelerate the racket forward to hit a serve or forehand.

You can perform isotonic exercises with body weight, free weights such as dumbbells or barbells, medicine balls, rubber tubing, and weight machines. Although there is no one best form of isotonic exercise for the tennis player, each form has advantages and disadvantages. For example, body weight is always available, you carry it with you wherever you go, but you cannot easily change your body weight as you get stronger to provide greater resistance.

Using free weights is a cost-effective form of training that requires great control during lifting because there is no guided path or movement track like a weight machine offers. Using free weights forces you to stabilize the weight in all directions while moving it in the primary movement pattern. This works secondary muscle groups that stabilize the joints you are exercising, but requires greater skill and supervision due to less control. One additional benefit of many weight machines is their ability to vary the resistance during the exercise range of motion.

Another type of resistance athletes commonly use is rubber tubing or rubber cords. This form of resistance is desirable because it is cost effective, easy to travel with, and potent because the farther you stretch the cord the greater the resistance you generate.

Whatever type of isotonic exercise you do, the important factor is movement. The joints move, the muscles lengthen and shorten, and this mimics the actions you do when hitting a serve or ground stroke. Most exercises in this chapter are isotonic exercises for the tennis player. They use free weights, rubber tubing, and weight machines to provide you with a resistance-training program using whatever methods are available to you.

Isokinetic resistance training uses a constant velocity and changing amounts of resistance. It uses a highly technical and expensive machine that does not allow most players to include this form of resistance in their training. Isokinetic machines are used extensively in rehabilitating injuries and in research, and they have given sport scientists important information regarding the strengths and weaknesses of the musculo-skeletal system of the tennis player.

Within each type of resistance for increasing strength there are two primary forms of exercise. These two forms are single-joint and multiple-joint exercises. In a *single-joint* exercise the athlete is exercising one primary joint and muscle group. For example, a knee extension exercise involves movement only at the knee joint and works primarily the quadriceps (front thigh) muscle. A *multiple-joint* exercise is one that works many muscles and muscle groups and includes movements at several joints simultaneously. A squat is a multijoint exercise that works the gluteals, quadriceps, hamstrings, calf muscles, and others, with movement occurring at the hip, knee, and ankle joints. See figure 3.2a and b for an illustration of human musculature.

Both types of exercise are beneficial to the tennis player. Multiple-joint exercises work more muscles and joints simultaneously and certainly are time efficient. Multiple-joint exercises such as the squat and lunge require great balance. Proper form and training are essential to achieve the optimum benefit and prevent injury. Single-joint exercises are beneficial when one muscle group is weak and the player has a muscle imbalance requiring exercise for one muscle group.

POWER TRAINING FOR TENNIS

Training the muscular system for power involves intense, explosive contractions that are performed rapidly, because power is speed applied to strength. Because of the increased risk of injury, we do not advocate using traditional exercise patterns with weight machines and free weights and simply performing them with fast, uncontrolled movements. Instead, players should use special types of resistance training to improve power in tennis.

One primary type of resistance training for power in tennis is *plyometrics*. Plyometrics were initially used as a method for improving explosive power in Eastern Europe and now have become a popular training method throughout the world. Plyometrics condition the body through dynamic resistance training that follows a specific pattern.

Plyometric exercises begin with a rapid stretching of the muscle, using an eccentric muscle contraction. This is immediately followed by an explosive shortening of the muscle (concentric contraction). A classic example of a plyometric exercise would be a box jump. A player stands on a wooden or metal box about 18 inches high, jumps off the box, and upon contacting the ground reverses his or her direction to jump as high as possible into the air. The time between the muscles lengthening, or eccentric contraction, and the shortening contraction is termed the *amortization* phase. The shorter this time or phase is, the more explosive or intense the plyometric program is.

The goal of plyometrics is to train the muscles and nervous system to react quickly to the stretch of the muscle by shortening the muscle at a maximal force and speed. Plyometrics have been used for many years to induce explosive strength and power in sprinters and other athletes.

Plyometric actions in tennis are everywhere. Think of your leg during a recovery step following a wide forehand. As your leg swings to contact the ground, your body weight transfers over it and stretches the thigh muscle to absorb the momentum. Then your muscles immediately shorten to recover and propel your body back into the court to continue playing the point.

Another example is the abdominal muscles during a serve. As your arm reaches behind you, your back arches or extends, stretching the abdominal muscles. As your shoulder and arm explosively rotate forward to contact the ball, your abdominals are shortening, as in a plyometric exercise. The eccentric contraction prestretches the muscle and surrounding tissues; enables an explosive, concentric contraction; and provides a training stimulus to increase strength.

Power training for tennis uses these plyometric movements. Athletes use on-court, tennis-specific drills and box jumps for the lower body and medicine balls for the upper body and trunk. You can safely perform explosive movement patterns using medicine balls, which allows you to train with plyometrics in an exciting, tennis-specific way.

RESISTANCE-TRAINING ADAPTATIONS

We can break down adaptations to resistance training into two forms—nervous system and muscular development. Improvements involving the nervous system can occur in as little as two weeks after starting a resistance-training program. When you begin lifting weights, and feel stronger after a week or two, this is primarily because the nervous system becomes more efficient in how it recruits or talks to the muscle. This in turn makes you feel stronger, even though little change has occurred within the muscle itself.

The second type of adaptation to strength training involves muscular adaptation. Scientists are still debating about the exact mechanism of this adaptation. Regardless of how it works, scientists agree that it takes at least six weeks for muscular adaptations to occur with training. Strength-training programs lasting 6 to 24 weeks will increase the percentage of lean body mass (muscle, bone, etc.) and result in a lower percentage of body fat.

One common myth about lifting weights for tennis is that it will make an athlete bulky and muscle-bound and will have a negative effect on foot speed and tennis strokes. This could happen, but only if you don't follow a strength-training program specific to tennis players. A tennis-specific strength-training program does not involve heavy, maximal effort lifts but instead uses light to moderate resistance levels with high repetitions that build strength and muscle endurance, not bulk and size.

Another myth associated with resistance training is that it will cause stiffness and loss of flexibility. Again, a program specifically for the tennis player, with a total conditioning program of flexibility (outlined in chapter 3), will prevent flexibility loss, optimize performance, and prevent injury.

DESIGNING A STRENGTH-TRAINING PROGRAM

Developing a needs analysis is the first step in designing a strength-training program for any athlete. Figure 4.1 outlines some necessary elements to determine what needs an athlete has, based on the demands of the sport.

The concept of specificity is vitally important when designing your training program. Every resistance exercise program must address the demands of the activity and consider the biomechanical requirements of

Roetert and Ellenbecker performed a biomechanics study to determine the racket head velocity during the first and second tennis serves in elite junior players. They found that the racket head velocity remained the same during the two serves. Contrary to what is often believed, biomechanical analysis showed that the racket moves about the same speed during first and second serves, meaning the muscles must work just as hard during both serves to produce and maintain the racket head speed.

Needs analysis

Exercise movements

- Muscles used
- Joint angles
- Contraction type (eccentric or concentric)

Energy system (metabolism) used

- Estimated contribution from aerobic/anaerobic metabolism
- Work:rest cycles, performance duration, frequencies

Injury prevention

- Most common sites (shoulder, trunk, elbow, knee)
- Player's history of injury

Figure 4.1   Athletic needs and demands for tennis.
Adapted by permission from S.J. Fleck and W.J. Kramer, 1997, *Designing Resistance Training Programs*, 2nd ed. (Champaign, IL: Human Kinetics), 89.

the sport. Biomechanical analysis helps sport scientists tailor training programs to tennis players. For example, by analyzing the tennis serve, scientists found that the shoulder is raised to little more than a 90-degree angle with the body at ball contact. The reason the racket looks so high over a player's head during the serve is that the trunk is bent to allow the shoulder to remain about 90 degrees and still hit the serve with maximum efficiency. Knowing this information leads us to recommend shoulder exercises that do not raise the arms higher than shoulder level.

Components of a Strength-Training Program

In designing a training regimen for tennis, consider the following components:

- Sets—groupings of repetitions within a resistance-training program. Typically multiple sets of an exercise are required to improve strength and muscular endurance. For tennis, we recommend two to four sets.

• Repetitions—the number of repetitions you perform per set. This determines the amount of work and regulates the exercise intensity. Exercise sets with three to six repetitions normally develop power and strength when you use higher resistance loads. Sets of 10 to 15 repetitions also develop muscular strength, as well as local muscle endurance due to the higher number of repetitions per set. Sets with 20 to 25 repetitions would train for endurance and are geared for an endurance athlete such as a marathon runner.

• Intensity—how much weight you lift. You set the exercise intensity using the *repetition maximum*, or RM system. This involves selecting an appropriate weight for an exercise set so you can perform all the desired repetitions without breaking proper form, and so you feel significant fatigue within the muscle during the last one or two repetitions of that set. For example, choosing a two-pound weight to do 10 repetitions of a biceps curl would probably not provide enough resistance to cause fatigue by the ninth or tenth repetition. A 50-pound weight would be far too heavy to perform 10 repetitions of the biceps curl unless you were Arnold Schwarzenegger. To properly apply the repetition maximum system takes some trial and error when beginning a strength-training program because the goal is specific: to choose a weight or resistance with which you can perform the preset number of repetitions, not break form, yet fatigue the muscle.

What is the optimal number of repetitions in a set for a tennis player? Most experts recommend sets ranging from 10 to 15 repetitions. This number provides a strength-training stimulus, as well as endurance, both of which are required for tennis. Using a high number of repetitions also means the relative amount of weight you use is lower because you must be able to do many repetitions with that weight.

• Movement cadence—speed. The speed that you move the weight has a tremendous effect on workout quality. We have all seen people working at the gym with too much weight, moving the weight rapidly from start to finish just to get their repetitions in. It is important that you emphasize a slow, controlled movement when you work on weight machines, free weights, and rubber tubing. This will ensure that you are raising and lowering, or pushing and pulling the weight, which means you will be working the muscle in both the shortening (concentric) and lengthening (eccentric) phase, similar to tennis play.

• Frequency—how often you do sessions. Typically, strength-training programs recommend rest between sessions of exercise. Depending on what other elements a player is emphasizing in the total conditioning program, the training frequency can range from one time per week to three or four times per week. Most strength-training programs recommend three times per week to build strength, with a day of rest between training sessions. Some players may lift weights every day, but they alternate what muscle groups and body areas they work to allow a day of recovery for the working muscles.

• Rest—time between sets. One factor closely tied to specificity is rest. In tennis, the average point lasts less than 10 seconds, followed by 25 to 30 seconds of rest. Therefore, a tennis player's program should emphasize rest periods of approximately 25 to 30 seconds between sets. This work:rest cycle provides a stress to the muscles similar to that in tennis play, and it metabolically stresses the systems that provide energy to the working muscles as if you were playing.

Strength-Training Workouts

With the essential design elements in mind, let's look at putting them into workouts. Be aware of these three points:

• Don't lift immediately before you play tennis. You don't want to be fatigued while you perform skilled motor tasks such as ground strokes. It is better to strength train on days when tennis workouts are lighter, and you can lift weights following your tennis.

• The status quo doesn't cut it with strength training. Every good program must be updated, following the principle of overload. If you always use a two-pound weight when doing 10 repetitions of a biceps curl, that will in time become too easy. To avoid training at an intensity level that is too low, add resistance when you no longer fatigue at the end of an exercise set. Some athletes increase the number of repetitions by three to five with the same weight; then when that becomes easy, they go back down to the original number of repetitions per set, but with a heavier weight.

• Avoid compensation. If you use too much weight, you will use bigger muscle groups and improper movement patterns that might produce injury. Stay within your limits of resistance, not your friends' or opponents' levels!

LOWER BODY MACHINE EXERCISES

LEG PRESS

Focus: Multiple-joint training exercise that works the gluteals, quadriceps, hamstrings, and calves.

Starting Position: Lie on your back adjusting the seat/sled to a position where your hips and knees are bent at 90-degree angles. Your feet should be approximately shoulder-width apart.

Exercise Action: Straighten your knees and hips by pressing down into the platform until they are almost completely straight. Do not lock your knees. Slowly return to the starting position.

*A variation of this exercise can be performed with only one leg at a time to focus on each leg independently. A second variation includes placing a six-to-eight pound medicine ball between the knees and squeezing the medicine ball as you straighten your knees and hips.

LEG EXTENSION

Focus: Single-joint exercise emphasizing quadricep strengthening.

Starting Position: Sit on the machine adjusting the backrest (if available) to such a location that the center of your knee is aligned with the rotating axis of the device. Your knee should be bent approximately 90 degrees and the resistance pad should be positioned just above your ankle.

Exercise Action: Extend your legs upward against the resistance, straightening your knees fully. Do not hyperextend your knees. Slowly lower the weight to the starting position.

Note: If you have knee pain or a history of knee problems, see chapter 10 for specific modifications of this exercise.

HAMSTRING CURL

Focus: Single-joint exercise that primarily works the hamstrings.

Starting Position: Lie on your stomach on the machine. The resistance pad should be adjusted such that it hits you on the lower third of your calf just above the ankle.

Exercise Action: Slowly curl your feet toward your buttocks. Slowly return the weights to the starting position. Your knees should not hyperextend in the starting position.

*A variation of this exercise includes bringing the weight up with both legs and then lowering the weight with one leg, alternating legs on every other repetition.

MULTI-HIP

Focus: An important exercise that works the stabilizing muscles around the hip and groin.

Starting position: Stand facing the machine, adjusting the height such that the machine's axis is aligned with the front of your hip. By adjusting the bar to a 45 degree angle, hip adduction (bringing your leg across your body) can be performed. A vertical adjustment of the bar allows the athlete to perform hip abduction (raising the leg away from your body), as well as hip flexion. Hip extension can be performed by placing the bar in a horizontal orientation and pushing the bar backward.

Exercise Action: In all four directions of movement, the stabilizing leg is working to balance the body, while the exercising leg is moving. Be sure to exercise both legs on this important machine.

LOWER BODY FREE-WEIGHT EXERCISES

STEP-UP

Focus: Multiple-joint exercise that emphasizes the quadriceps, gluteals, and calf musculature.

Start Position: Stand with a medicine ball placed behind your neck and stabilized with your hands or holding dumbells at your sides.

Exercise Action: Using a six- to eight-inch step, alternately step up. Vary this exercise by stepping forward, to the side, and crossing over to step up onto the platform.

SQUAT

Focus: Multiple-joint training exercise that works many muscles, including the gluteals, quadriceps, hamstrings, back extensors, and calves.

Starting Position: Stand with your feet parallel to your shoulders (the feet may point slightly outward), with dumbbells in your hands resting at your sides or a medicine ball placed behind your neck and stabilized with both hands.

Exercise Action: Bend your legs in a slow, controlled manner until your knees are at a 90-degree angle, with your thighs parallel to the ground. As you bend, keep your head up looking straight ahead, chest out, and back flat. Keep your weight back toward the middle and rear of your feet, not on your toes. Return to the starting position, keeping your head up and back flat.

Note: If you have knee problems or a history of knee problems, bend your knees only 45 to 60 degrees, as you can tolerate (see chapter 10, Knee Injuries).

LUNGE

Focus: A multiple-joint exercise that works most muscles in the lower extremities and trunk. It is a tennis-specific movement pattern.

Starting Position: Stand with your feet six to eight inches apart, holding a dumbbell or placing a medicine ball comfortably behind your neck and stabilizing it with both hands.

Exercise Action: Take a large step forward and position your body over your front leg. Bend your front knee so it is in line with or slightly in front of the ankle joint and does not project beyond a line drawn up from the front of your shoe. Return to the starting position by pushing your weight backward and straightening your front leg. You may need to take a few small steps to return your leg to the starting position. Keep your trunk erect during the exercise by looking straight ahead and keeping your chest out. Alternate legs.

Lunge (variation 1): Crossover lunge—Instead of stepping forward, move your front leg in a 45-degree diagonal (moving the left leg in a crossing direction in front of your right leg and foot). Alternate between the right and left legs, using this crossover diagonal pattern.

Lunge (variation 2): Side lunge—Step directly to your right or left side, sinking into a squat position as shown. Alternate between the left and right sides. If you have knee problems, you will want to bend the knee only 30 to 45 degrees to decrease stress.

LEG RAISE WITH CUFF WEIGHTS

Focus: A single-joint exercise that works the hip flexors and quadriceps.

Starting Position: Lie on the back with elbows on the ground and cuff weights at the ankles. Bend the non-exercising knee 90 degrees.

Exercise Action: With the knee straight, tighten the thigh muscles. With thigh muscles tight, raise the leg off the floor approximately six to eight inches. Hold for one to two seconds and lower leg to floor. Relax three to five seconds and repeat 20 to 30 times.

CALF RAISE

Focus: Develops the gastrocnemius and soleus (calf) muscles.

Starting Position: Stand with your feet six to eight inches apart, holding dumbbells in each hand or placing a medicine ball comfortably behind your head and stabilizing it with both hands.

Exercise Action: Keeping your knees straight and trunk upright, raise your heels off the ground until you are standing on the balls of your feet. Slowly return to the starting position. Move through as large a range of motion as possible. Begin this exercise standing flat on the floor, and progress to performing it with your toes on a step or on the platform of an exercise machine. This position allows the heels to drop below the balls of the feet when you start and allows you to exercise through a larger range of motion.

TRUNK

CRUNCH

Focus: Develops power for all strokes. A strong trunk (rectus abdominis) is the source of many movements and allows the upper body to stay synchronized with the lower body.

Starting Position: Lie on the back with the knees bent and feet flat on the floor. Hold your hands behind the head with the elbows to the sides, or crossed resting on top of your chest. Refrain from pulling the head forward with the hands.

Exercise Action: Curl the upper body from the floor, including the head and the shoulders, until you can feel the abdominal muscles contracting. The upper body should be off the ground by about three inches at the shoulder blades. Lower until the shoulder blades touch the ground and repeat.

CROSSOVER CRUNCH

Focus: Strengthens the internal and external oblique muscles of the trunk. They are responsible for trunk rotation.

Starting Position: Lie on the back with one knee bent and the foot flat on the floor. The opposite knee is bent so the heel rests on the other knee. Hold your hands behind the head with the elbows out to the sides. Refrain from pulling the head forward with the hands.

Exercise Action: Curl the upper body so the elbow opposite the elevated knee moves toward it diagonally. Repeat this movement on the opposite side.

SEATED TRUNK CIRCLES

Focus: Develops the entire abdomen and trunk. This exercise requires more strength than the basic abdominal exercises.

Starting Position: Lie on the back with the hips and knees bent at 90 degrees. Hold your arms and hands behind the head with elbows out to the sides. Refrain from pulling the head forward with the hands.

Exercise Action: Touch the left elbow to the right knee and vice versa. Alternate touches without allowing the knees to rest.

REVERSE SIT-UP

Focus: Works the rectus abdominis through a full range of motion with little use of the iliopsoas (hip flexors).

Starting Position: Lie on the back, raise your feet and place them on a box or bench. Hold your hands behind the head with elbows out to the sides. Refrain from pulling the head forward with the hands.

Exercise Action: Curl the body up and attempt to touch the chest to the thighs.

HIP RAISES

Focus: Develops rectus abdominis strength.

Starting Position: Lie on the back with the hips elevated and legs straight in the air. Place arms and hands out to the sides for stability or under the lower back for support.

Exercise Action: Raise the hips off the ground and point the toes toward the ceiling while flexing the abdominal wall. With control, lower the hips to the ground and repeat.

DIAGONAL SIT-UP

Focus: Targets the oblique muscles of the trunk.

Starting Position: Secure your feet on the floor, with the knees bent and the body flat against the floor. Place both arms on the same side and hold the racket in the hands.

Exercise Action: Bring the arms up and across the body by using the trunk to raise and twist to the opposite side. Perform a diagonal movement, alternating sides.

SIT-UP WITH LEGS RAISED

Focus: Develops the rectus abdominis and iliopsoas.

Starting Position: Lie on the back with hips and knees raised at 90 degrees. Hold your hands behind the head with elbows out to the sides. Refrain from pulling the head forward with the hands.

Exercise Action: Curl the upper body from the floor, including the head and the shoulders, until you can feel the abdominal muscles contracting. The upper body should be off the ground by three inches at the shoulder blades. Lower until the shoulder blades touch the ground and repeat.

ROTARY TORSO MACHINE

Focus: Strengthens the internal and external obliques.

Starting Position: Position the seat so you have approximately 90 degrees of hip and knee bend. Set the rotation to allow a 60- to 90-degree arc of movement.

Exercise Action: Press into the upper body pad with your shoulder, rotating your trunk to one side. Slowly return to your starting position and repeat. Do rotations to both sides to promote balanced trunk rotation strength.

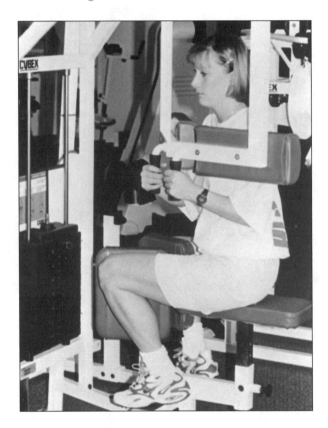

RUSSIAN TWIST

Focus: Works the obliques of the trunk.

Starting Position: Secure feet against the floor, with the knees bent and the body leaning back at a 45-degree angle. Hold the arms straight out from the shoulders so they are parallel with the thighs. Holding a racket increases the resistance of the exercise.

Exercise Action: Rotate side to side, turning the shoulders until the arms are at a 90-degree angle with the body. Make a full twist to the opposite side. Over and back makes one repetition.

HIP ROTATION

Focus: Develops strength in the rectus abdominis, obliques, and iliopsoas.

Starting Position: Lie on the back with the hips flexed and knees extended. Place arms and hands out to the sides for stability.

Exercise Action: Rotate the hips and trunk to one side until they touch the ground. Keeping the knees together, rotate them all the way over until they touch on the other side. You have done one full rotation when you have touched both sides.

TRUNK EXTENSION

BACK EXTENSION MACHINE

Focus: Strengthens the erector spinae and gluteal muscles.

Starting Position: Align your hips with the machine axis, and secure your position with a safety belt or harness if available. The starting position is normally in about 45 degrees of trunk flexion (bending).

Exercise Action: Cross your arms over your chest and move your spine back against the resistance pad until it is completely straight. Return to the starting position slowly, working the muscles of the low back eccentrically.

SUPERMAN

Focus: Helps prevent overuse injuries or chronic low-back pain by targeting the erector spinae muscles along the spinal column.

Starting Position: Lie prone on the floor with arms fully extended overhead.

Exercise Action: Lift both arms and both legs simultaneously. Hold this position for one to five seconds and return to the start position. A variation might include lifting the right arm and the left leg, followed by lifting the left arm and right leg in an alternating pattern.

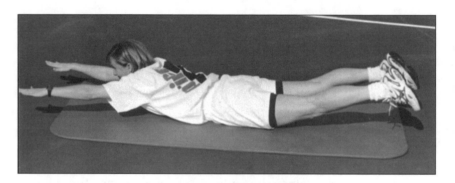

HYPEREXTENSIONS

Focus: Strengthens the erector spinae. Allows the lower back to absorb and exert greater forces during such actions as the service motion and overhead.

Starting Position: Lie on the abdomen on a table with the trunk and upper body hanging off the end. Hold your hands behind your head. Have a partner hold down your lower body.

Exercise Action: From a lowered starting position, raise the upper body until it is in line with the rest of the body or until the back is tight. Lower the upper body to a 30-degree angle or just before the lower back curves.

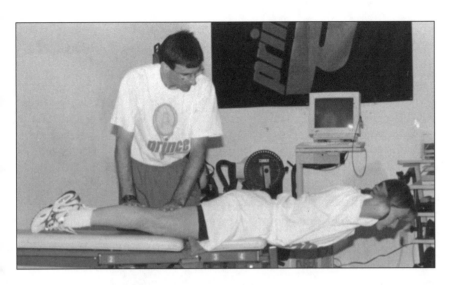

REVERSE HYPEREXTENSIONS

Focus: Strengthens the erector spinae to prevent injury and chronic back pain.

Starting Position: Lie on the abdomen on a table with the legs hanging off the end.

Exercise Action: While keeping the feet together, raise and lower the legs. Perform this slowly and repeat.

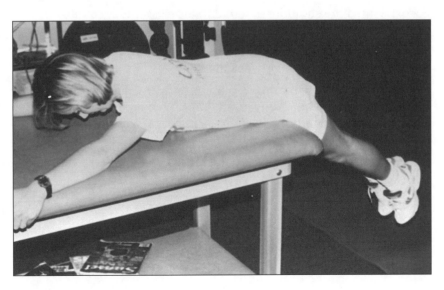

ROTATOR CUFF PROGRAM

The following exercises work the rotator cuff muscles. You should initially perform them with a one- or two-pound weight because these muscles are small. We recommend three sets of 12 to 15 repetitions to promote endurance to these muscles. If you use a heavier weight you may compensate and perform the exercise using larger muscle groups that are already developed. Even the strongest, largest athletes use a maximum of four or five pounds on these exercises.

EXTERNAL SHOULDER ROTATION

Focus: Develops rotator cuff strength.

Starting Position: Lie on the left side with the right arm at the side and a small pillow or towel tucked under it. Keep the right elbow bent at a right angle and fixed to the side.

Exercise Action: With the right hand near the abdomen, slowly raise the hand until the forearm is just short of vertical to the body. Slowly lower to the starting position and repeat. Note photo on page 188.

PRONE EXTENSION

Focus: Works the shoulder external rotators, scapular stabilizers, and posterior deltoid.

Starting Position: Lie on your stomach on a table with the racket arm hanging straight down toward the floor.

Exercise Action: With the thumb pointed outward, raise the arm straight back toward the hip. Slowly lower the arm and repeat. Do not raise the arm forward toward the head. Note photo on page 189.

PRONE HORIZONTAL ABDUCTION

Focus: Works the rotator cuff, rhomboids, trapezius, and posterior deltoid.

Starting Position: Lie on a table on your stomach with the racket arm hanging straight down toward the floor and thumb pointing outward.

Exercise Action: Raise the arm out to the side at a 90-degree angle until it is almost parallel to the floor. Lower it to the starting position and repeat.

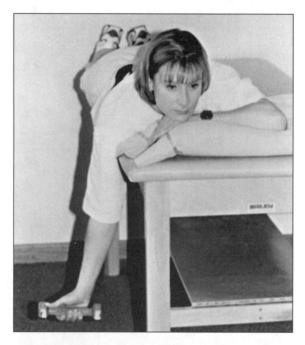

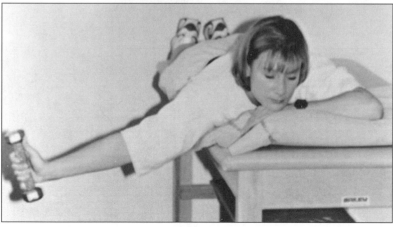

90-90 EXTERNAL SHOULDER ROTATION

Focus: Develops the shoulder external rotators.

Starting Position: Kneel with the arm on an incline bench. Place the upper arm parallel to the ground and the forearm perpendicular to the upper arm at 90 degrees.

Exercise Action: While maintaining a right angle at the elbow, externally rotate the forearm until it points to the ceiling (90-degree abduction). Slowly lower it and return to the starting position.

External Shoulder Rotation (variation): You can also perform this exercise lying on your stomach with the shoulder raised to a 90-degree angle, and elbow and hand hanging over the edge of the table. Raise the back of your arm toward the ceiling until it is parallel with the floor.

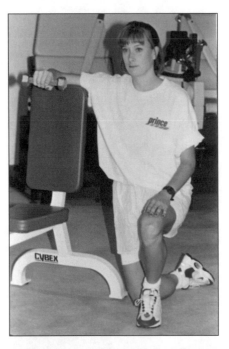

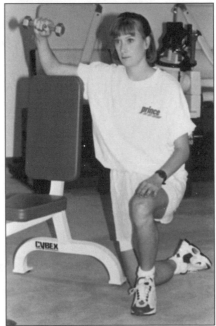

SCAPTION OR EMPTY CAN

Focus: Works the supraspinatus muscle and deltoid.

Starting Position: Stand with the elbow straight and thumb pointed to the ground.

Exercise Action: Raise the arm to shoulder level on a diagonal plane (30-45 degrees to the side, not straight out to the front). Slowly lower and repeat.

Note: Be sure you don't raise the arm past shoulder level.

ROTATOR CUFF PROGRAM WITH RUBBER TUBING

These exercises use rubber tubing or Thera-band. You can purchase this from physical therapy clinics and fitness distributors. You can use the medium (blue) or medium heavy (black) tubes for rotator cuff strengthening.

EXTERNAL SHOULDER ROTATION

Focus: Develops external rotation strength.

Starting Position: Secure the rubber tubing, about waist high, to a doorknob. Stand sideways to the door with the racket arm away from the door. Place a small, rolled towel under the racket arm.

Exercise Action: Hold the rubber tubing in the racket hand and start with the hand close to the abdomen. Rotate the hand and forearm away from the abdomen until the hand and forearm are straight out in front, pulling on the tubing for resistance. Return to the starting position and repeat. Keep your elbow at a 90-degree angle throughout the exercise. You can place your opposite hand under your elbow to support the arm if needed.

EXTERNAL SHOULDER ROTATION WITH ABDUCTION

Focus: Works the rotator cuff in a position specific to the tennis serve.

Starting Position: Secure the rubber tubing, about waist high, to a doorknob. Stand facing the door with your shoulder abducted 90 degrees, about 30 degrees in front of you on a diagonal. Use your opposite hand to support your upper arm.

Exercise Action: Hold the tubing in your hand and rotate your hand back until it reaches nearly vertical. Return to the starting position and repeat.

INTERNAL SHOULDER ROTATION

Focus: Develops internal rotation strength.

Starting Position: Secure the rubber tubing, about waist high, to a doorknob. Stand sideways to the door with the racket arm close to the door. Place a small, rolled towel under the racket arm.

Exercise Action: Hold the rubber tubing in the racket hand and start with the hand and forearm straight out in front of you. Rotate the hand in toward the abdomen. Return to the starting position and repeat. Keep your elbow at a 90-degree angle throughout the exercise. You can place your opposite hand under your elbow to support the arm if needed.

ADDITIONAL UPPER BODY EXERCISES

SEATED ROW

Focus:　Develops the rhomboids, trapezius, posterior deltoid, and biceps.

Starting Position:　Sit with your knees slightly flexed and your hands holding a cord or band device, cable column, or seated row machine.

Exercise Action:　While keeping the upper body erect and not leaning backward, pull band handles toward the chest and upper abdomen area. Keep the elbows close to your sides. Slowly return to start position and repeat.

BENT OVER ROW

Focus:　Develops the latissimus dorsi, rhomboids, trapezius, and posterior deltoid.

Starting Position: Bend over a flat bench, with the nonworking knee and hand resting on the bench. Keep your back in a flat, supported position by tightening the abdominals and buttocks.

Exercise Action: Begin with the dumbbell in hand and the arm fully extended below the shoulder. Lift the dumbbell by raising the elbow toward the ceiling. You have completed one repetition when the dumbbell touches the side of the abdomen.

PUSH-UPS

Focus: General upper body conditioning/strengthening exercise.

Start Position: Hands placed shoulder-width apart with your body in a straight line from your toes to your head.

Exercise Action: Slowly lower yourself down until your upper arm is parallel to the ground. Push yourself upward until the elbows are completely straight and round your back outward like a cat. This rounding motion at the end of the push-up is very important and increases the work by the muscles that stabilize your shoulder blade.

Note: If you have shoulder pain or a history of shoulder problems only lower yourself about one-half of the way down.

LAT PULL DOWN

Focus: Develops the latissimus dorsi and bicep muscles.

Starting Position: Using a lat pull down machine, overhead cable, or rubber tubing, reach upward to grasp the handles with a wide grip.

Exercise Action: Pull down on the bar, cable, or tubing, bringing the bar *in front of you* toward the middle of your chest. Slowly return the bar to the starting position with control and repeat.

CHEST PRESS

Focus: Develops the pectoralis major/minor, serratus anterior, triceps, and anterior deltoid.

Starting Position: Lie on your back on a narrow bench with the arms externally rotated at a 90-degree angle to the torso.

Exercise Action: While keeping the wrists directly over the elbows and not locking the elbows, extend the hands toward the ceiling. As you extend your hands upward, round your shoulders pushing your hands as far away from you as you can. This extra motion works the serratus anterior muscle, which supports your shoulder blade while you play tennis.

BICEPS CURL

Focus: Works the bicep brachi, brachialis, and brachioradialis.

Starting Position: Stand holding a dumbbell in your hand with your feet shoulder-width apart.

Exercise Action: Keeping your shoulder at your side, bend your elbow and bring the weight toward your shoulder. If you have chosen the weight correctly, you should not be arching your back or leaning backward during the exercise. Slowly return the weight to the starting position, making sure you don't hyperextend or lock your elbow.

TRICEPS EXTENSION

Focus: Develops the tricep muscle.

Starting Position: Lie on your back holding a dumbbell in your hand with your shoulder and elbow bent 90 degrees. Use your opposite hand to support your upper arm and keep it stationary throughout the exercise.

Exercise Action: Straighten your elbow by raising your hand and weight upward, making sure the elbow does not lock.

SHOULDER SHRUGS

Focus: Works the upper trapezius and scapular stabilizers.

Starting Position: Stand with feet shoulder-width apart, with your arms at your sides and holding dumbbells in your hands.

Exercise Action: Keeping your arms at your sides, raise your shoulders upward toward your ears; then squeeze your shoulder blades together while rolling your shoulders backward. Return to starting position by slowly lowering your shoulders and repeat.

SHOULDER PUNCHES

Focus: Develops the serratus anterior—an important scapula stabilizer.

Starting Position: Lie on your back with your shoulder flexed to 90 degrees and elbow straight. Hold a medicine ball or dumbbell.

Exercise Action: Keeping your elbow straight, raise your hand toward the ceiling as far as you can. Slowly return to the starting position. If you do this correctly, your hand will move only about six inches up and down.

PRONE FLYS

Focus: Develops the posterior deltoid, rhomboids, and trapezius.

Starting Position: Lie prone on a narrow bench with your feet off the ground.

Exercise Action: With dumbbells in hand, extend your arms from your sides at a right angle (90 degrees). While maintaining a right angle at the shoulder, raise your arms until they are nearly parallel to the ground.

FOREARM AND WRIST PROGRAM

WRIST CURLS: EXTENSORS

Focus: Develops the wrist and finger extensors.

Starting Position: Sit in a chair with the elbow flexed and forearm resting on a table or over your knee. Let the wrist and hand hang over the edge. Turn the hand so the palm is down.

Exercise Action: Stabilize the forearm with the opposite hand, and slowly curl your wrist and hand upward. Be sure to move only at your wrist, not at your elbow. Raise your hand slowly, hold for a count, and slowly lower weight. Repeat.

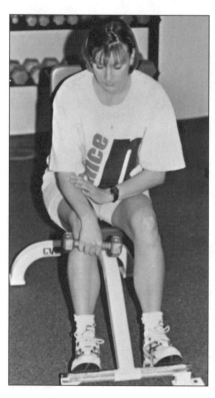 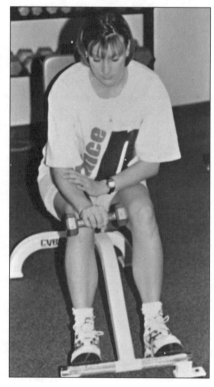

WRIST CURLS: FLEXORS

Focus: Develops the wrist and finger flexors.

Starting Position: Sit in a chair with elbows flexed and forearm resting on a table or over your knee. Let the wrist and hand hang over the edge. Turn the hand so the palm is up.

Exercise Action: Stabilize the forearm with the opposite hand, and slowly curl your wrist and hand upward. Be sure to move only at your wrist, not at your elbow. Raise your hand slowly, hold for a count, and slowly lower weight. Repeat.

FOREARM PRONATION

Focus: Develops the forearm pronators.

Starting Position: Sit in a chair with the elbow flexed and forearm resting on a table or your knee. Let the wrist and hand hang over the edge. Using a dumbbell with a weight at only one end (i.e., a hammer), begin the exercise with the palm upward so the handle is horizontal.

Exercise Action: Slowly raise the weight by rotating your forearm and wrist to the upright (vertical) position.

FOREARM SUPINATION

Focus: Develops the forearm supinators.

Starting Position: Sit in a chair with your elbow flexed and forearm resting on a table or your knee. Let the wrist and hand hang over the edge. Using a dumbbell with weight at only one end (i.e., a hammer), begin the exercise with the palm down.

Exercise Action: Slowly raise the weight by rotating your forearm and wrist to the upright position. Hold for a count, then slowly return to the starting position.

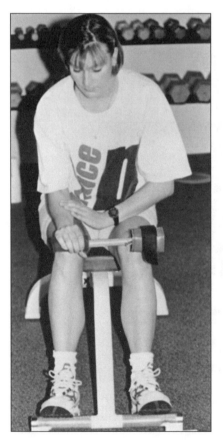 

RADIAL DEVIATION

Focus: Develops the muscles that stabilize the wrist during tennis.

Starting Position: Stand with your arm at your side and grasp a dumb-bell with weight on only one end. The weighted end should be in front in the neutral position (thumb pointing straight ahead of you).

Exercise Action: Slowly raise and lower the weight through a comfort-able range of motion. All the movement should occur at the wrist with *no* elbow or shoulder joint movement. You will not be able to exercise through a large arc of movement. Repeat.

ULNAR DEVIATION

Focus: Develops the muscles that stabilize the wrist during tennis.

Starting Position: Stand with your arm at your side, and grasp a dumbbell with weight on only one end. The weighted end should be behind your exercising hand.

Exercise Action: With your forearm in the neutral position (thumb pointing straight ahead of you), slowly raise and lower the weight through a comfortable range of motion. All the movement should occur at your wrist with *no* elbow or shoulder joint movement. You will not be able to exercise through a large arc of movement. Repeat.

GRIP STRENGTHENING

Focus: Develops the forearm, wrist and hand muscles needed to grip the tennis racket.

Starting Position: Begin with your elbow bent 90 degrees at your side. Hold a tennis ball or putty in the palm of your hand.

Exercise Action: Squeeze the ball or putty firmly and hold three to five seconds. Release pressure and repeat until you feel fatigue. Progress to performing this exercise with the elbow straight.

BODY WEIGHT PROGRAM

You can perform these exercises simply by using your body weight. We recommend them for young players who have never started a resistance training program and for players who travel and do not always have access to equipment or free weights.

Note: You can find the descriptions and instructions for the following exercises on the page numbers listed in parenthesis.

- Squats (p. 74)
- Step-ups (p. 74)
- Lunges (p. 74)
- Sit-ups (p. 78)
- Superman (p. 82)
- Push-ups (p. 91)

PLYOMETRIC MEDICINE BALL PROGRAM

These exercises develop power in the upper body. They use a medicine ball for resistance and require explosive movement patterns. Typically, you can do them with a four- to six-pound medicine ball. You can increase the weight of the ball when the workout becomes too easy. Begin with sets of 20 to 25 repetitions of each exercise, and advance to performing sets until you fatigue. If you can perform more than 50 repetitions without fatigue, you should increase the weight of the ball.

CHEST PASS

Focus: Works the pectorals, triceps, and scapular stabilizers.

Starting Position: Stand 8 to 10 feet from a partner. Hold the ball in front of the chest.

Exercise Action: Pass the ball to the partner. When you receive the ball from your partner, try to catch and release it back to your partner as quickly as possible.

OVERHEAD TOSS

Focus: Develops the latissimus dorsi and tricep muscles.

Starting Position: Stand 8 to 10 feet from your partner. Hold the medicine ball directly over your head.

Exercise Action: Toss the ball to your partner. When you receive the ball from your partner, try to catch and release it back to your partner as quickly as possible.

FOREHAND TOSS

Focus: Develops the muscles used in the forehand.

Starting Position: Stand 8 to 10 feet from your partner. Hold the ball with both hands at your forehand side.

Exercise Action: Step and turn, just as you would to hit your forehand, taking the ball back like a racket. Pass the ball to your partner, mimicking a crosscourt forehand ground stroke. When you receive the ball from your partner, try to catch and release it back to your partner as quickly as possible.

BACKHAND TOSS

Focus: Develops muscles used in the backhand.

Starting Position: Stand 8 to 10 feet from your partner. Hold the ball with both hands at your backhand side.

Exercise Action: Step and turn, just as you would to hit your backhand, taking the ball back like a racket. Pass the ball to your partner, mimicking a crosscourt backhand ground stroke. When you receive the ball from your partner, try to catch and release it back to your partner as quickly as possible.

WOOD CHOPS OR SIDE THROWS

Focus: Emphasizes trunk rotation and development of the obliques and rectus abdominus.

Starting Position: Stand 8 to 10 feet from your partner, facing sideways. Hold the ball at shoulder height with both hands.

Exercise Action: Throw the ball using a sideways and slightly downward movement pattern to your partner. When you receive the ball from your partner, try to catch and release it back to your partner as quickly as possible.

SEATED TRUNK TWISTS

Focus: Develops the trunk musculature: rectus, erector spinae, and obliques.

Starting Position: In a seated position, hold the ball directly in front of you with both hands.

Exercise Action: Place the ball gently on the ground directly behind you. Quickly rotate your trunk to the opposite side and retrieve the ball with both hands. Repeat this movement for the desired number of repetitions; then reverse the direction.

STANDING TRUNK TWISTS

Focus: Develops the trunk and lower back musculature: rectus, erector spinae, obliques, and gluteals.

Starting Position: Stand back to back with a partner, with one or two feet between you and your partner.

Exercise Action: Hand the ball to your partner by rotating to the right and your partner rotating to the left. The partner then takes the ball and rotates to the opposite side as you receive the ball by rotating to your left. Continue this pattern for a desired number of repetitions; then repeat this exercise by changing directions.

Note: A progression of this drill includes both partners rotating to the same side simultaneously and handing the ball off directly behind you. This requires more rotation and a larger range of motion.

SIT-UPS WITH PARTNER TOSSES

Focus: Develops the rectus abdominis using a more explosive power-oriented format.

Starting Position: Lie on your back with your knees bent 90 degrees and feet on the floor. Hold a medicine ball in both hands over your chest. Have a partner standing three to five feet from your feet.

Exercise Action: Sit up and pass the ball to your partner as you come up. Continue the upward motion of your sit-up, and instruct your partner to pass the ball to you as you return to the starting position. Try to absorb the weight of the ball without gaining speed.

CIRCUIT TRAINING FOR TENNIS

The traditional strengthening exercises that we presented in this chapter can provide a comprehensive stimulus to develop muscular strength and endurance. Adding exercises to a basic program helps prevent boredom, and can boost the motivation and effort you put into training. One such alternative exercise regimen is circuit training.

Circuit training combines muscular strength and endurance exercise with a cardiovascular (aerobic) training component. Circuit training uses stations that include calisthenics, free weights, weight machines, and plyometrics. Using these training stations creates a type of interval training, with work:rest intervals of approximately one:one. The short rest periods and work intervals stress the cardiovascular system, in addition to providing a strength and endurance stimulus to the muscular system. Typical sets and repetitions used in circuit training are as follows:

Repetitions: 8 to 12*

Sets: 2 or 3

Rest: 30 to 45 seconds

*You can use time intervals of 30 to 45 seconds of exercise in place of repetitions.

Typically 10 to 15 stations are used in a circuit-training program, with two or three work periods at each station. See chapter 9 for sample programs. The advantage of adding a circuit-training program to your strength-training program is to include cardiovascular and muscular strength benefits and add variety to your training schedule.

CHAPTER 5

AEROBIC AND ANAEROBIC TRAINING

Many tennis players will vividly recall Pete Sampras' path to winning the 1996 U.S. Open Championships. Pete endured five set matches, illness, extreme heat and humidity, and all the stresses that a Grand Slam tournament entails. Pete's ability to sustain excellent performance over the two-week tournament ultimately led to his victory in the finals. Success in tennis demands high levels of cardiovascular fitness, and players must include activities that enhance their cardiovascular fitness in their complete conditioning program.

Optimal tennis performance requires great intensity with powerful bursts of activity, as well as stamina and endurance over a long match or practice session. Due to these characteristics, tennis players must have good aerobic and anaerobic fitness. Match analyses indicate that more than 300 to 500 energy bursts are required during a tennis match. To train these important energy systems, you must understand the concepts and characteristics of the anaerobic and aerobic energy systems.

AEROBIC AND ANAEROBIC BASICS

The energy that the body uses to perform comes from two sources: aerobic (with oxygen) and anaerobic (without oxygen). Aerobic activity includes longer duration and steady-paced movements that require the body to receive energy from burning carbohydrates and fats using aerobic energy pathways. Anaerobic activity is a high-intensity, short-duration event that uses energy stored in the muscles or made rapidly when you initiate the activity.

The body's heart rate is lower during aerobic exercises than during the more maximal level anaerobic exercises. Truly aerobic activities, such as running a marathon or swimming long distances, use primarily aerobic energy sources, which provide the body with the ongoing energy it needs to continue performing. Aerobic exercise uses fat as a fuel source and is important in an exercise program geared to affect body composition. Aerobic exercise, with a fat-reduced diet, can decrease the amount of body fat and positively affect a player's body composition.

For continuous training activities such as slow-paced jogging, the amount of anaerobic energy you use is about 5 percent, with 95 percent

© Russ Adams Productions, Inc.

coming from aerobic energy production. Sprinting uses only 5 percent aerobic and 95 percent anaerobic energy.

Tennis is different from running or swimming in that it combines the short bursts of activity—requiring maximum effort, with high heart rates—allowing only brief rest periods for recovery. Playing tennis relies on both aerobic and anaerobic energy pathways for a continuous energy supply. This energy allows a player to function at strong intensities during points (anaerobic), as well as recover and repeat these bouts several times during a match or practice session (aerobic).

TENNIS—AEROBIC AND ANAEROBIC

Research performed on tennis players during singles practice and match play has consistently rated tennis as a prolonged, moderate intensity exercise activity. One indicator used to measure exercise intensity is heart rate.

Activities are rated as a percentage of the individual's maximal heart rate. We can measure this directly by performing a treadmill or bicycle ergometer maximal stress test, which incrementally increases the exercise intensity until the athlete cannot continue. The heart rate in beats per minute at the time of exhaustion from the exercise workload is the maximal heart rate. We can also estimate the maximal heart rate value using the following equation when scientific testing is not practical: Maximal heart rate = 220 – (athlete's age).

Using the formula for a 20-year-old tennis player would result in a maximal heart rate of 200 beats per minute. We would then express exercise intensities as a percentage of the maximal heart rate. Figure 5.1 shows the average maximum heart rate for adults. Maximum heart rate does decline with age and has some variability based on training and fitness levels as indicated by the shaded region on the chart.

For tennis players the exercise intensity level ranges between 60 and 90 percent of the maximum heart rate during play. This would mean that while the 20-year-old was playing tennis, heart rate would range between 120 and 180 beats per minute. This heart rate intensity classifies tennis as an activity that would meet the American College of Sports Medicine's requirement for improving cardiovascular fitness. Tennis includes repeated high-intensity bouts of exertion while maintaining a moderate overall intensity throughout performance. Therefore it consists of both aerobic and anaerobic demands. Figure 5.2 displays common percent breakdowns of sport activities, all of which have a continuum of aerobic and anaerobic energy demands.

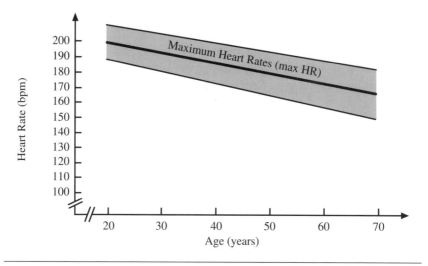

Figure 5.1 Average maximum heart rate.
Reprinted by permission from B. Sharkey, 1985, *Coaches Guide to Sport Physiology* (Champaign, IL: Human Kinetics), 92.

ANAEROBIC AND AEROBIC ENERGY PRODUCTION

Based on the physiology of tennis, a player must have both aerobic and anaerobic fitness to play at his or her highest level. What does this mean? *Anaerobic* literally means "without oxygen" and refers to the energy systems used by the body to produce energy units called ATP. To a tennis player, ATP typically stands for the Association of Tennis Professionals, but to exercise physiologists and other sports scientists ATP stands for Adenosine Tri-Phosphate, which is a high-energy compound used by muscles and other body tissues to function. ATP is required for every activity the body does, whether it's breathing, beating the heart, or contracting muscles to hit a backhand.

Anaerobic energy production or metabolism involves two systems. The first and most immediate is called the ATP-PC system. This consists of stored energy within the muscles and working tissues and is immediately available when we start an activity. For example, hitting a serve would use stored energy in the muscle, because it only takes seconds.

The muscle can store a limited amount of ATP, and the anaerobic system can immediately produce approximately 6 to 10 seconds of maximal intensity work. After approximately 10 seconds of intense work, the predominant energy system the body uses is *anaerobic glycolysis*. Glycolysis involves breaking down the carbohydrate from our diet

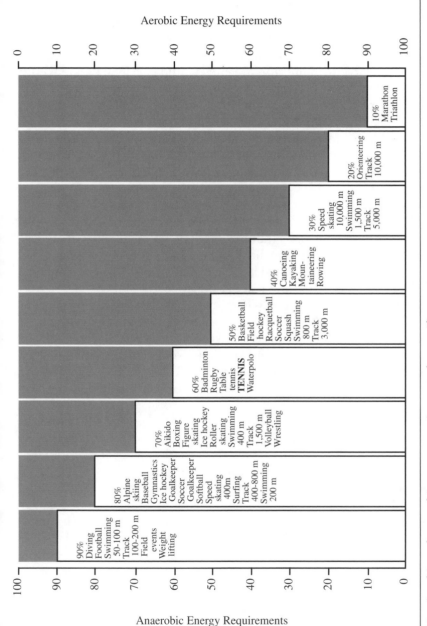

Figure 5.2 Aerobic and anaerobic energy requirements for specific sports.

Adapted by permission from B. Sharkey, 1985, *Coaches Guide to Sport Physiology* (Champaign, IL: Human Kinetics), 100.

through a complex chemical conversion. Energy in the form of ATP is produced without the presence of oxygen.

A by-product of anaerobic glycolysis is lactic acid, which is formed during the production of ATP using this system. With continued high-intensity muscle work, lactic acid accumulates in the muscle, and the athlete must stop due to the burning sensation from the lactic acid. An example of lactic acid buildup in tennis would be a long baseline rally between two players. The heavy, burning sensation in the quadriceps (thigh muscle) that you feel as you move explosively between forehands and backhands is from lactic acid accumulation.

Anaerobic glycolysis is only an effective energy source for high-intensity exercise lasting at most two or three minutes. At that time exercise activity must either stop or be lowered in intensity so the next energy system can produce energy for more prolonged activity. Performing on-court agility and power drills (such as those in chapters 6 and 7) can improve your energy production using this system and build a tolerance to lactic acid. By training, the body becomes better at quickly removing the lactic acid from the working muscles during recovery. This rapid removal of accumulated lactic acid allows top players to continue playing after only 30-second rest periods in tennis.

The final energy system we will discuss is the aerobic energy system. As its name implies, the *aerobic* energy system requires oxygen taken in through the lungs and carried to the working tissues in the bloodstream to produce energy. In the presence of enough oxygen, the aerobic energy system is the most efficient producer of ATP for the body and is the primary energy system for long, endurance sport activities, such as running a 10K or a marathon.

To provide you with a continuous supply of energy or ATP, the body uses all the energy systems we mentioned in this chapter. Figure 5.3 shows how the body's energy systems work together for continuous energy production overlapping during activities.

Applying the energy system continuum to tennis is easy, and it helps explain why both anaerobic and aerobic conditioning are necessary for enhancing tennis performance. Because tennis involves repetitive muscular contractions and exertion, the aerobic system provides the baseline energy during a tennis match and or practice session. Aerobic fitness is important for recovery following a strenuous baseline rally, bursts of movement, and maximal skills such as executing a serve and volley sequence or an overhead.

We need anaerobic energy production for maximal activities during points. Testing performed by the USTA on elite tennis players indicates high levels of aerobic fitness (treadmill test, endurance run) as well as superior anaerobic power (sprinting and agility tests). This

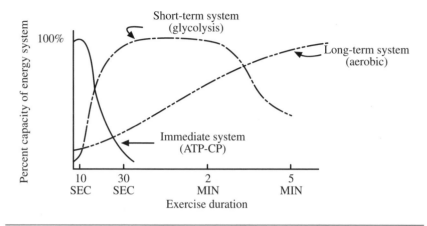

Figure 5.3   Energy production during exercises of different durations.
Reprinted by permission from McArdle, Katch, and Katch, 1981, *Exercise Physiology: Energy, Nutrition, and Human Performance* (Philadelphia: Lea and Febiger), 134.

explains a player's ability to maximally sprint from side to side during a baseline rally, and after 25 seconds rest, do it again. Athletes with better aerobic fitness levels can clear the accumulated lactic acid from the working muscles more rapidly than individuals with less aerobic fitness. Likewise, athletes with greater anaerobic power capability can run faster and jump higher because of more energy stores in the trained muscle.

ANAEROBIC TRAINING FOR TENNIS

In tennis matches the average point lasts 5 to 10 seconds. The average rest most players take is 18 to 20 seconds, with a maximum allowable rest time between points being 25 seconds. This creates a work:rest cycle. A one:two work:rest cycle represents the physiological activity pattern during tennis.

In addition to the work:rest cycle, we often apply the term specificity. Specificity involves the athlete's training being similar to the demands in their sport.

Anaerobic training techniques in tennis use both the work:rest and specificity concepts. Recommended drills and activities that improve anaerobic power follow the one:two work:rest cycle and include short, multidirectional movement patterns. The following list includes examples of how we can apply specificity with anaerobic tennis training:

Specificity Training Concepts

- A tennis point usually contains four to five directional changes.
- Most tennis points last less than 10 seconds.
- Tennis players always carry their rackets during points!
- Players seldom run more than 30 feet in one direction during a point.
- Movement patterns contain acceleration and controlled deceleration.

Tennis-specific drills to improve on-court movement and footwork as well as anaerobic power are included in chapter 7. Any exercise activity that includes a short period of maximal intensity work, followed by a period of rest or recovery that is two or more times longer than the work period would stress the anaerobic energy system.

Recommended *general* anaerobic training drills for tennis include the following:

- Wind sprints
- Line drills
- Side shuffles
- Alley hops
- Kangaroo hops
- Cariocas
- Ladder drills

You should perform these general anaerobic training drills with a tennis racket in hand to make them more specific for tennis.

Specific anaerobic training drills for tennis include the following activities (adapted from Loehr, *USTA Sport Science for Tennis Newsletter* - Spring 1991, White Plains, NY: USTA, 4):

1. *A hitting partner or coach to feed balls.* One coach can conduct this training sequence for a maximum of two players at once.

2. *One hour of workout time.* Each person will drill for one hour. If you have a hitting partner, alternate every 30 minutes. You will need a two-hour time block.

3. *A minimum of 80 balls or 160 if a coach is working with two players.*

4. *A stopwatch.*

5. *Realistic feeding.* Remember the average distance covered per point is only 60 feet; therefore, feeding continuously from corner to corner is unrealistic. Feeding rate should be approximately 1.3 seconds per feed. At that rate, feeding 15 balls should take around 20 seconds. The feeder can vary the ball placement based on the

needs of the player. A waist-high ball basket will assist the coach with feeding. The player should not know how many balls will be fed during each point, thus simulating match situations.

6. *Targets.* These designate hitting areas; use cones, ball cans, or boxes.

7. *The player is to hit balls at designated target areas.*

8. Except for warm-up, the player is to complete the entire series at *maximum intensity.*

9. The feeder should follow a *predetermined schedule of exercise and rest intervals* spaced every 10 to 15 minutes, with 90-second breaks for the player to sit down, drink, and towel off. The player must sit down. See figure 5.4 for a sample work:rest exercise agenda.

10. *Heart rate monitor* (optional). Take heart rates before and after 90-second breaks to gauge workloads, intensity levels, and recovery rates.

Work (W)/Rest (R) Interval Schedule				
Series 1 * W/R	Series 2 W/R	Series 3 W/R	Series 4 W/R	Series 5 W/R
1 2/15	7/20	8/20	3/25	7/20
2 6/15	2/20	8/20	3/25	5/20
3 3/15	2/20	8/20	3/25	1/20
4 10/15	16/20	8/20	3/25	10/20
5 8/15	4/20	8/20	3/25	6/20
6 ** 2/15	6/20	8/20	3/25	3/20
7 7/15	1/20	8/20	3/25	2/20
8 15/15	12/20	8/20	3/25	7/20
9 4/15	9/20	8/20	3/25	16/20
10 3/15	3/20	8/20	3/25	4/20

*** 90-second sit-down break between each series

*   "W" is the number of balls to feed (work) and "R" is the number of seconds of recovery (real).

** Feeds 6 through 10 should occur in each series only after the player has served the ball.

*** During the 90-second break, the feeder must pick up the balls and prepare for the next series. The feeder must also record heart rates before and after the break.

Note: Whenever possible, record the number of balls hit outside the designated target areas. The goal is to keep errors to a minimum during all sequences.

Figure 5.4   Work:rest exercise agenda.
Adapted, by permission, from Loehr, USTA *Sport Science for Tennis Newsletter* Spring 1991, White Plains, NY: USTA, 4.

AEROBIC TRAINING FOR TENNIS

For an exercise activity to stress the aerobic system, tennis players need to adhere to several basic concepts. Aerobic exercise training activities typically involve large major muscle groups, are repetitive, and include continuous repeated or cycled exertion. Examples of this are running, swimming, stair climbing, sliding, and biking.

Additional characteristics of aerobic exercises include frequency, duration, and intensity. One key document referenced when recommending aerobic exercise is produced by the American College of Sports Medicine (ACSM). Their general guidelines for improving aerobic fitness with exercise are as follows:

Duration: Minimum of 20 to 30 minutes of continuous exercise

Frequency: Minimum of three times per week

Intensity: 60 to 85 percent maximum heart rate

© Russ Adams Productions, Inc.

Improving and maintaining aerobic fitness levels is an important part in the overall training program for tennis players. We recommend identifying players with low levels of aerobic fitness using the fitness testing guidelines in chapter 2. Depending on the degree of need in the individual's training program, aerobic exercise is an important activity to include. Several factors are important to consider before adding aerobic training to a player's program.

- **Timing.** We do not recommend fatiguing a player with aerobic exercise before a skill practice session. Do aerobic training after skill-oriented, tennis-specific training and on days of light training of other components.

- **Frequency.** Similar to other types of exercise training, start aerobic training gradually, for example, one or two times per week along with other training activities, and progress based on the athlete's individual needs.

- **Variety.** Choose an aerobic training activity that best suits the player. Adding distance running to a training program of a player with a history of knee or lower extremity injury may not be as appropriate as cycling, slideboard exercises, or swimming. Use cross-training with aerobic training to avoid boredom, encourage multiple muscle group development, and increase enjoyment.

- **Testing.** Finally, use testing to measure aerobic fitness levels and gauge improvement (see chapter 2). Excessive aerobic training may invite overuse injuries and take precious training time from anaerobic training and skill-oriented tennis training.

To be successful in tennis, you must include both aerobic and anaerobic fitness training in your program. Using these general and specific guidelines and understanding the principles of how the body produces and uses energy is of utmost importance.

CHAPTER 6

QUICKNESS AND AGILITY DRILLS

Mary Joe Fernandez has excellent
anticipation, but in addition she exhibits tremendous balance while she
moves toward each shot. One of the reasons she hits each ball so cleanly
is that she is perfectly balanced and set up before making contact with
the ball. She has great control over her center of gravity.

One important thing in becoming a good tennis player is to be in the
correct position to hit the ball. You must not only have good footwork so
you can get to the ball, but also have proper balance once you get there.
Keeping your body and racket under control while you are moving is
often referred to as dynamic balance. To have a stable base of support,
the feet should be underneath you and approximately shoulder-width
apart. Of course this is not always possible, especially when you get
pulled wide on a shot. The trick is to keep control of your center of
gravity as much as possible while you are playing.

© Russ Adams Productions, Inc.

The *center of gravity* is the point about which your body balances most perfectly. For example, pick up a pencil and hold it across your finger so it balances. The point where the pencil stays without falling is its center of gravity.

The center of gravity in males is usually a little higher than in females. During a point in a match, your center of gravity may even fall outside your body at certain times. Reaching or lunging for shots pulls the body off balance and slows the next movement, which keeps you from producing power on your shots. Keeping the center of gravity in line with your base of support provides optimum balance, and lowering your center of gravity makes you more stable.

The following quickness and agility drills will help develop your dynamic balance and control your center of gravity while improving your movement skills. You can perform these drills at the end of each practice or training session.

GENERAL MOVEMENT DRILLS

W-DRILL

Purpose: Simulates backpedaling for an overhead, shuffling, then sprinting for a short ball.

Set-Up: Start at the left net post facing the net.

Action: Backpedal from the net post to the corner of the singles sideline and baseline, then side shuffle to the T and continue shuffling to the other corner of the singles sideline and baseline. From there sprint to the right net post.

Key Point: You can also perform this drill in a team competition.

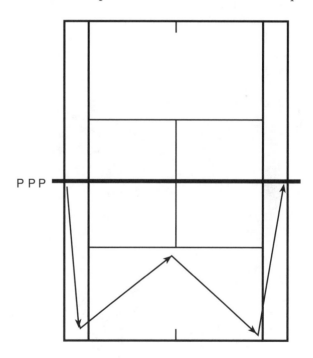

LADDER RUNS

Purpose: Improves footwork by having players stay on their toes.

Set-Up: Lay out a ladder on the court. If a ladder is not available, you can use a series of rolled-up towels.

Action: Run through the ladder, making sure to touch each space.

Key Point: Quickness is the key, so focus on touching down as lightly as possible.

Ladder Runs (variation 1): You can also perform this drill by touching every other space or even every third space. In addition, you can do a side-facing crossover or carioca step.

Ladder Runs (variation 2): You can also perform this drill by starting behind and to the left of the ladder. Starting with the right foot, followed by the left, place two feet in the first space; then put the right foot outside the ladder. Put two feet inside the second space (left foot first); then put the left foot outside the ladder. The third space has the same sequence as the first. Continue this pattern until you reach the end of the ladder.

© Lance Jeffrey

ALLEY HOPS

Purpose: Plyometric drill to increase leg strength.

Set-Up: Start at the baseline behind the alley and face the net.

Action: Hop from side to side, touching the doubles sideline with the right leg and singles sideline with the left leg. Continue this pattern, moving forward all the way to the net. Try to touch down as lightly as possible each time.

Key Point: Some player's legs aren't long enough to touch both sidelines. The important thing is the movement skill. Don't be concerned if you can't reach both sidelines.

Alley Hops (variation): You can also perform this drill using a deeper knee bend and holding that position for one second on each hop.

SUICIDES

Purpose: Helps develop quick stops and starts.

Set-Up: Stand on the side of the court facing the doubles sideline.

Action: Touch each line, then return to starting doubles sideline.

Key Point: You can use two courts side by side to increase the difficulty.

Suicides (variation): You can also perform this drill using a lateral shuffle or backpedaling to the starting point after you touch each line. This is a great drill for large groups and can be performed as a relay race. To make sure each line is touched, pick up balls at each line and place them back at the starting point.

CONE DRILLS

CONE HOPS

Purpose: Builds explosive leg strength.

Set-Up: Align three cones approximately two feet from each other.

Action: Hop forward with both feet together over all three cones.

Key Point: You can increase the distance between the cones as you improve.

Cone Hops (variation): You can also perform this drill by hopping sideways and by going in both directions. An advanced version of this drill is to hop on one leg only. Adequate leg strength and balance are a prerequisite.

THE EXCHANGE

Purpose: Helps develop a quick first step and a quick direction change.

Set-Up: Place two cones at the center of the baseline and one at the center of the service line.

Action: Start on the baseline, pick up one of the cones, and prepare to sprint to the service line. On "go," sprint to the service line and exchange cones. Place the first cone down before picking up the second one. Repeat this action by sprinting back to the baseline and exchanging the cones there. Time this action for 30 seconds, and count the number of pickups for your total score.

Key Point: You can also perform this drill by sprinting forward toward the service line and backpedaling toward the baseline.

THE SIDEWINDER

Purpose: Stresses the importance of a crossover step after shuffling along the baseline.

Set-Up: Arrange three cones on the baseline with one cone in the center and the other cones three feet on either side of it.

Action: Start at one end and begin weaving through the cones, using a side-shuffle movement. At the end of the cones, take a crossover step and sprint to the doubles sideline. After touching the sideline, return by shuffling along the baseline and weave through the cones in the opposite direction. Then take a crossover step and sprint to the opposite sideline.

Key Point: Tennis is a sport that combines shuffling and sprinting toward the ball. Focus on a quick burst of speed after the shuffle.

THE SNAKE

Purpose: Improves lateral movement.

Set-Up: Arrange six cones three feet apart along the baseline.

Action: Start at one end and weave through the cones using a lateral shuffle. Circle the last cone and weave back to the starting point.

Key Point: Complete this pattern three times and record time.

The Snake (variation): Repeat the pattern from the previous drill, but after weaving through once, sprint forward and perform a split step at the T. Then backpedal to the opposite side of the cones in the starting area and repeat the pattern two more times.

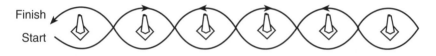

TEAM DRILLS

TENNIS TAG

Purpose: Players practice all the right tennis moves in a fun environment.

Set-Up: All players spread out on one side of the court within the boundaries of the singles lines. A designated tagger stands in the middle. Players may not leave the court area during the drill.

Action: The tagger tries to tag as many players as possible. As soon as someone is tagged they have to leave the court. The last person left wins the game.

Key Point: If it gets too difficult to tag the last one or two people, you can change the boundaries to include only the two service boxes.

LATERAL DIRECTION CHANGE

Purpose: Works on quick changes of direction similar to the movement during a baseline rally.

Set-Up: All players should face their coach or partner, who stands with back to the net on the same side of the court.

Action: Shuffle sideways until you hear the command "change," at which point immediately start shuffling in the opposite direction.

Key Point: Simulate a long point by following this pattern for 10 to 20 seconds, then take a 30-second rest.

Lateral Direction Change (variation 1): Shuffle in the same pattern, but occasionally a partner will call out a player's name. That player has to circle the coach as quickly as possible and go back to the original position.

Lateral Direction Change (variation 2): Instead of the players shuffling in both directions, hop on one leg (for example, hop on the right leg while moving to the right or hop on the left leg while moving to the left).

Lateral Direction Change (variation 3): The partner can stand behind the players to give them an auditory cue only.

© Lance Jeffrey

THE WHEEL

Purpose: Simulates sprinting for a ball, followed by a direction change.

Set-Up: All players are on the same side of the net. Set up a cone at the T as the center of the wheel. An equal number of players line up behind each other in four spots on the court, two groups at the ends of the baseline (one at each end) where it meets the doubles sideline and the other two groups at each net post.

Action: The first player from each group sprints toward the cone, touches it, and proceeds to where the next group stands (moving clockwise), touches that station, and sprints back to the cone again. Follow this pattern until the players return to where they started. As soon as the first player reaches the starting point, the next player in line takes off.

Key Point: This can be a competitive event to see who can catch the team ahead of them.

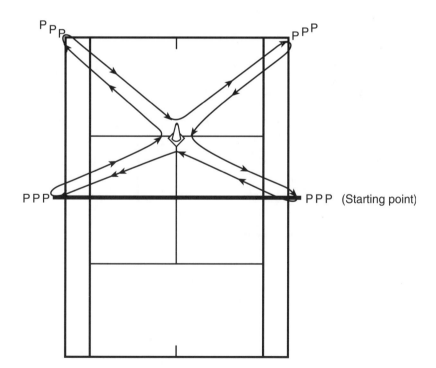

X-DRILL

Purpose: This drill involves several direction changes and movement patterns.

Set-Up: Two teams compete against each other. The teams are on opposite sides of the net. The players line up behind the first player in line, at the corner of the baseline and doubles sideline. The teams are directly across from each other.

Action: At the command "go" the first player from each line shuffles along the baseline to the opposite doubles sideline. As soon as the players touch this line they sprint diagonally to the net post. From there the players shuffle along the net (players from both teams should be facing each other at this point) to the other net post, turn, and sprint diagonally to the starting point. The next player in line starts as soon as the first player crosses the finish line.

Key Point: You can perform this drill with or without racket in hand. The drill is most fun if both teams are relatively equal.

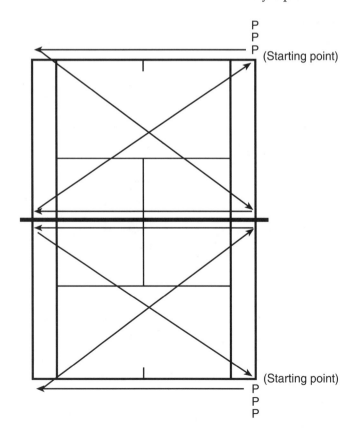

CHAPTER 7

BALL AND RACKET DRILLS

Tennis is often described as a game

of continual emergencies, because with every shot the opponent hits, a ball could have a different velocity, a different type or amount of spin, and land in a different part of the court. Therefore, speed and agility are crucial to good court movement and correct positioning on the court. Fast lateral movements occur frequently in a tennis match, and you are often forced to stop this movement in one step to prepare for the following stroke. Tennis depends on quick bursts of speed, interspersed with slow gliding steps. In other words, to strike the ball effectively in tennis, your body must be properly positioned, which requires using legs and feet. So, while your arm uses the racket to *hit* the ball, your legs get you in *position* to use the racket.

© Russ Adams Productions, Inc.

Although a mixture of quickness and agility drills is preferable, the most effective drills are those performed on the court using a racket and tennis balls. Especially during the precompetitive and competitive phases of periodization training (see chapter 8), the goal is to modify training routines to approximate the demands of competitive tennis. On-court drill work should involve high-intensity, explosive exercises matched closely to competitive play.

The following quickness and agility drills simulate movement skills used in match play and require using a tennis racket or balls. As with the general speed and agility drills in chapter 6, these drills are great to end a practice session with, although sometimes you may want to build a whole practice around improving your movement skills.

MOVEMENT DRILLS WITH TENNIS BALL

FOLLOW THE BALL

Purpose: Improves movement in all directions.

Set-Up: Your coach or partner stands with ball in hand, across the net facing you.

Action: As your partner or coach holds the ball in clear view and moves it side to side and forward and backward, you follow the pattern by moving in the designated direction.

Key Point: Don't anticipate, instead focus on reacting as quickly as possible to the movement of the ball.

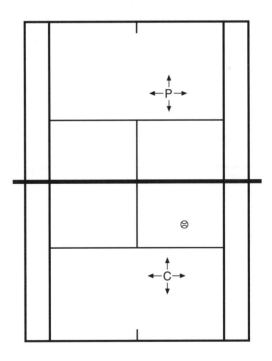

THE BALL AND THE WALL

Purpose: Helps develop eye-hand coordination.

Set-Up: Stand facing a wall with a coach or partner right behind you. The distance to the wall will vary depending on your skill level. Start at 10 feet and move closer as your skill improves.

Action: Your partner tosses the ball against the wall, and you catch the ball on the rebound.

Key Point: You can increase the difficulty of this by tossing the ball harder, standing closer to the wall, or designating which hand will catch the ball.

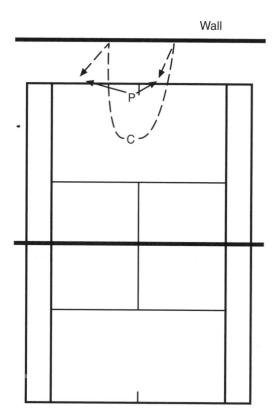

TURN AND SEARCH

Purpose: Teaches quick recognition and improves first step toward the ball.

Set-Up: Stand about 10 feet in front of your coach or partner with your back turned.

Action: Your partner tosses the ball up in the air and calls out "turn" as the ball is about to bounce. Turn, find the ball, and catch it on one bounce.

Key Point: You can increase the difficulty of this drill by tossing the ball lower, having your partner stand farther from you, or calling out the command "turn" later.

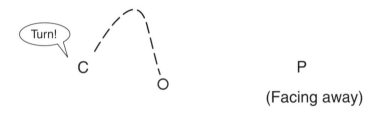

(Facing away)

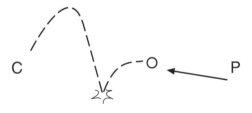

ROLL AND TOSS

Purpose: Improves lateral movement and speed in direction change.

Set-Up: Coach or partner kneels at the T, facing you on the baseline at the same side of the net.

Action: Your partner rolls a ball to either side of you. Shuffle laterally, retrieve the ball, and toss it back to your partner. Then change direction to retrieve the ball coming to the opposite side and toss it back to your partner. Drill continues for 6 to 10 repetitions.

Key Point: Keep the chin up and back straight, and bend at the knees not the waist.

Roll and Toss (variation 1): Repeat the drill with the partner adding the command "go." React by running forward to touch your partner's hand; then backpedal to the baseline to continue.

Roll and Toss (variation 2): Repeat the drill, but at the "go" command, run forward, circle around your partner, and backpedal to the baseline to continue.

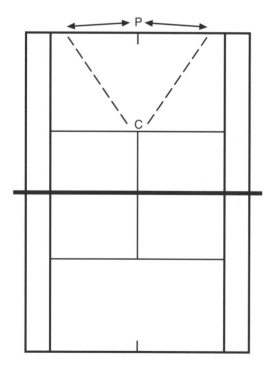

JUGGLING AT THE NET

Purpose: Improves eye-hand coordination and quickness at the net.

Set-Up: Face your partner while on opposite sides of the net.

Action: Your coach or partner tosses balls alternately to forehand and backhand sides. Catch each ball with the right hand on the forehand side and the left hand on the backhand side, while stepping across with the opposite foot. As soon as you catch the ball, toss it back to your partner.

Key Point: Your partner should have several balls in hand to be able to speed up the action once you have mastered the pattern.

Juggling at the Net (variation): Repeat the drill with your partner tossing an occasional lob. Retrieve the ball on the bounce, toss it back to your partner, and continue the drill.

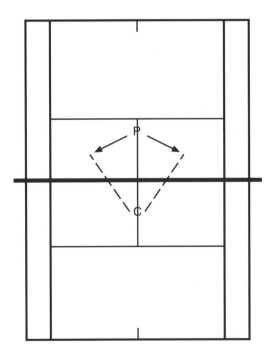

BALL DROPS

Purpose: Develops explosive first step toward the ball.

Set-Up: Your coach or partner stands between baseline and service line with one ball in each hand and arms extended to the side. Stand on the baseline facing your partner.

Action: Your coach or partner drops either one of the balls and you try to catch it before it bounces a second time.

Key Point: Your partner can make the drill more difficult by standing farther from you.

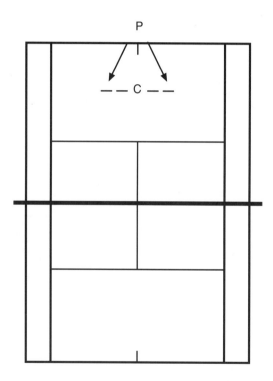

MONKEY IN THE MIDDLE

Purpose: Improves response time and focus on the ball.

Set-Up: Two players stand approximately 16 feet apart, with you standing halfway between them.

Action: The other players alternately toss balls to you. You react to the command "turn" by immediately turning around and catching a ball tossed underhand by the person who's behind you. As soon as you catch and toss the ball back, wait for the command from the next player.

Key Point: Focus on being on your toes. The other players can speed up the tempo to make the game more challenging.

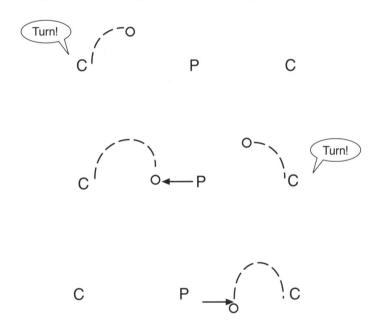

GLIDE AND CATCH

Purpose: Improves response time and quickness at the net.

Set-Up: You and your coach or partner are at the net on opposite sides. Your partner has several balls in hand and you have your back to the net.

Action: Your partner tosses balls as both you and your partner shuffle alongside the net. At the command "turn," turn and catch the ball, and immediately turn back to face the baseline. When you get to the opposite side doubles sideline, shuffle back the other way while keeping the drill going.

Key Point: Work on staying in a proper ready position while shuffling. Your partner can mix in high and low balls.

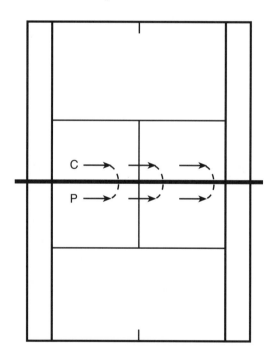

MOVEMENT DRILLS WITH RACKET

PLYO GROUNDIES

Purpose: Develops an explosive first step along the baseline.

Set-Up: Set up two barriers on the baseline near one sideline. Your coach or partner stands facing you at the same side service line with several tennis balls in hand.

Action: Hop over barriers, feet together until landing the second time. On the second landing split step, turn, sprint to the opposite sideline, and hit a ground stroke. Your partner tosses the ball as you split step.

Key Point: Work this drill on both forehand and backhand sides to see which side is stronger.

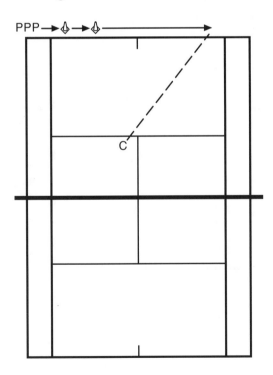

FOREHAND ONLY

Purpose: Improves lateral movement along the baseline.

Set-Up: Stand in the ready position in the center of the baseline. Your coach or partner feeds from the other side of the net.

Action: Your partner runs you from side to side, but you are only allowed to hit forehands. Your partner can designate either cross-court or down-the-line targets.

Key Point: This is an excellent drill to work on the inside-out and inside-in forehands.

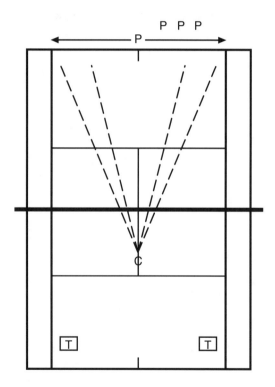

DOUBLE DROP DRILL

Purpose: Improves lateral movement and teaches you to cut the ball off at an angle.

Set-Up: Stand in the ready position in the center of the baseline. A partner or coach stands in each doubles alley, three feet inside the baseline with three balls in hand.

Action: Shuffle along the baseline, until the designated partner (e.g., the forehand-side partner) calls "change" to make you change direction, or "forehand," or "backhand." The corresponding (forehand or backhand side) partner will drop a ball from shoulder height. After hitting the ground stroke, recover near the center of the baseline. Partners in the alley who are dropping the ball can vary their positions closer to the baseline or service line.

Key Point: Emphasize balance on the split step and an explosive first step toward the ball.

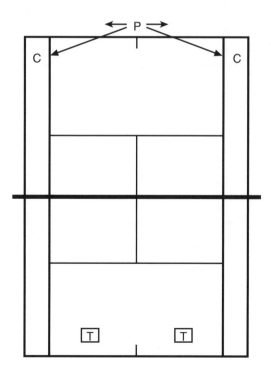

WRONG FOOT DRILL

Purpose: Improves lateral movement and direction change.

Set-Up: Stand in the ready position in the center of the baseline. Partner or coach feeds from the other side of the net.

Action: Your partner runs you from side to side and tries to wrong foot you.

Key Point: Your partner can call out the direction or target of the desired shot.

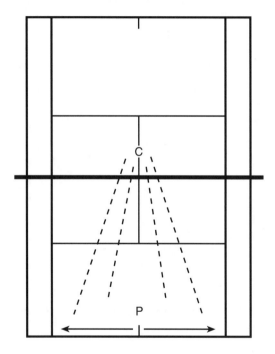

TRANSITION DRILL

Purpose: Works on hitting a variety of shots as you advance to the net to close out the point.

Set-Up: Your coach or partner feeds balls rapidly from the opposite side baseline.

Action: Shuffle along the baseline; then sprint forward to the center service line, split step, and hit a forehand volley. Follow this immediately by a backhand volley while closing in to the net. The final shot in the sequence is an overhead while backing up.

Key Point: Replicates a common pattern of play.

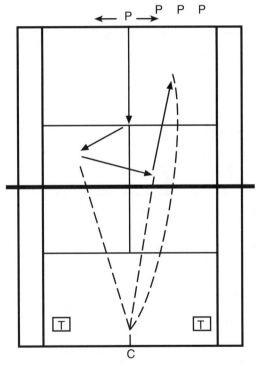

(Right-handed player)

TURN, TURN, TURN

Purpose: Reinforces rotating the body and preparing early for ground strokes.

Set-Up: Stand on the baseline in one of the alleys with a coach or partner facing you. Set up a cone crosscourt in the corner as a target.

Action: Your partner drops six balls, one at a time, while backing up slowly toward the net. Alternate hitting forehands and backhands aiming at the target crosscourt.

Key Point: Quick footwork is necessary here. Concentrate on rotating fully to prepare for the next shot. As you approach the net, adjust the angle of the shot.

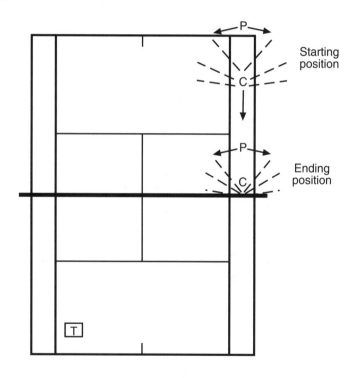

HI-LO DRILL

Purpose: Teaches you how much reach you have at the net, while taking only one step in each direction.

Set-Up: Your coach or partner feeds from opposite side service line while you are at the net.

Action: Alternate hitting a high forehand volley with a low backhand volley for a series of 10 shots each. After a short rest, reverse the sequence to a high backhand and a low forehand volley.

Key Point: Work on proper body rotation while alternating hitting the volleys.

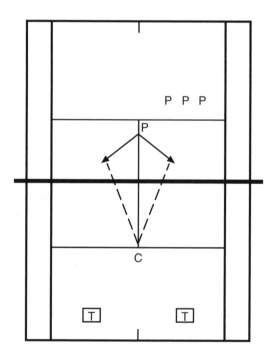

PLYO VOLLEYS

Purpose: Develops an explosive first step at the net.

Set-Up: Set up two cones in line with the center service line, one on each side of the T. Your coach or partner stands on the opposite side of the net facing you and tosses the ball as you split step.

Action: Jump with both feet over the first barrier and immediately over the second barrier, landing in a split step. As you split step, your partner tosses ball to either side for a forehand or backhand volley.

Key Point: This is a plyometric drill; therefore, you should spend minimal time on the ground. Emphasize first-step explosiveness reacting to the ball toss.

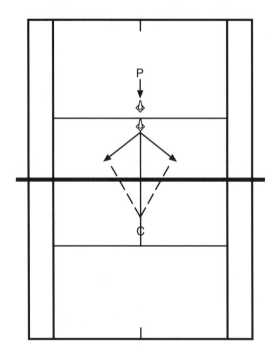

CLOSE AND DROP

Purpose: Works on both forward and backward movement and reinforces closing-in while at the net.

Set-Up: Your coach or partner kneels at the net facing you on the same side service line. Set up two cones on the other side of the net as targets for the drop shots.

Action: Your partner alternates tossing balls to left and right sides, forcing you to sprint up and hit a drop shot. After each shot, backpedal as quickly as possible to the starting position (the center of the service line). Perform for 30 seconds, then rest for 30 seconds while another player performs the drill.

Key Point: Vary the length of the drill, or make the work:rest ratio similar to a tennis point.

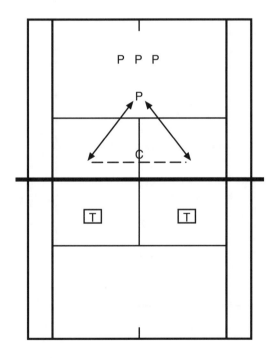

PROTECT YOUR TURF

Purpose: Improves movement skills around the net.

Set-Up: Stand in the center of one service box. Your coach or partner stands with a basket of balls on the opposite side of the net.

Action: Your partner feeds balls rapidly from the opposite side service line, moving you back and forth and side to side within the service box and alley. If there is more than one player, the second player quickly jumps in when you miss.

Key Point: Split step to change direction quickly. This can also be a good doubles drill, with one player in each service box and one player at each net post waiting to jump in when the player on their side misses.

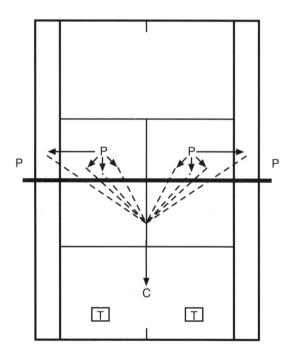

CHAPTER 8

DESIGNING A TRAINING PROGRAM

Whether you're an elite professional tennis player like Anna Kournikova or Malivai Washington or a serious recreational tennis player trying to improve your game and conditioning level, one common obstacle stands in your way: *time!* How do you organize a training schedule to improve flexibility, aerobic conditioning, anaerobic power, muscular strength, and endurance and still play tennis? That is what the next two chapters will tell you. First, we discuss the basic components you need to design a program; then, in chapter 9, we provide sample programs for tennis players to use as templates for designing an optimal program for your game.

Step number 1: Have a plan! An important aspect of designing a comprehensive training program is having a focused plan or set of goals. Some sport science experts call this a needs analysis. No player, whether a professional athlete who has all day to devote to the game or a recreational player who has to balance family, job, and other responsibilities, has time to do all components of a training program every day.

© Russ Adams Productions, Inc.

In addition to time limitations, the body has its own limitations. To optimize the time you spend training for tennis and minimize the risks of overtraining, such as burnout, fatigue, and injury, you must formulate a plan to prioritize and identify key areas of need.

One recommended way to formulate your plan is to use what the experts use—fitness testing. In chapter 2 we outlined groups of tests that you can do with little or no equipment to identify your skill or fitness level in the major categories of fitness: flexibility, strength, agility, and anaerobic and aerobic conditioning.

Using testing to highlight the specific areas accomplishes two goals. Number one, you immediately know what areas you need to work on, and number two, you can gauge your improvement as you train. This means you will be able to update or change your program as you continue to train. Using the testing protocol and results provided in chapter 2 will provide you with an ideal start in designing your complete conditioning program and will highlight the areas you need to emphasize to improve your game and fitness levels.

Training Program Components

• Individuality—You should individualize a training program for your specific needs. Using the sport science testing approach is one sure way of making a self-tailored program.

• Specificity—Adaptations the body makes to training are specific to the type of training or stresses that the body encounters. Therefore, your program should be tennis specific (a sumo wrestler would perform different exercises and undergo different stresses than a tennis player). Throughout this text, we have provided examples of how the body is stressed in tennis, and the training programs listed in chapter 9 are tennis-specific, based on these stresses.

• Overload and adaptation—To enhance the body's strength or cardiovascular conditioning levels, we must apply an exercise stress or overload. An example of overloads in training programs would be using weights, or running stairs or hills. The nature of the overload you use determines the type and degree of the body's adaptation response. We use overloads specific to tennis players so the body will adapt in ways that enhance your tennis performance.

• Progression—If you follow a program such as those in chapter 9, the body will initially adapt to the loads and stresses of that program. However, if you do not progress the training, you will get no further gains or adaptations. Therefore, you must periodically progress your program so the body continues to improve and adapt to the new training loads.

• Overtraining and recovery—Overtraining occurs when the exercise overload is too stressful for the body to correctly adapt. Typical signs of overtraining are excessive fatigue, pain, emotional stress and irritability, and burnout. Overtraining doesn't just make you bored, it can make physiological improvements difficult, if not impossible. It produces tired, weak muscles, which at best will not grow and at worst will be at great risk for injury. To avoid overtraining you must increase training loads slowly, avoid heavy training on consecutive days, and use cross-training methods. Using recovery periods is the primary way of preventing overtraining. Athletes use a recovery period, sometimes hours, one day, or two weeks, to avoid tissue damage, overtraining, and prevent burnout. Following a proper periodization schedule will ensure that recovery is part of your program.

SETTING REALISTIC GOALS

In chapter 2 we present the fitness testing results using ranges from "excellent" to "needs improvement." As you can see in many categories, there are only small differences between excellent, average, or needs improvement. The reason for this is that fitness improvements do not always come quickly or overnight, and many times involve small changes in time, speed, flexibility, and so on. Using these charts will guide you in setting realistic goals. Don't expect to improve from the needs improvement category to excellent in two weeks. Instead, set small performance goals that you can attain incrementally as your training continues.

Be sure to set performance goals rather than outcome goals. An *outcome goal*, although attractive and inspiring, is not under your direct control and often is unattainable. An example of an outcome goal would be, "I will win the U.S. Open singles championship." Obviously this goal is not under your control and does not consider performances of other players and other elements. An example of performance goals would be, "I will be able to do 15 push-ups in one minute," "I will improve my aerobic fitness level so I am not tired in the third set of my tennis matches," and so on. *Performance goals* are under your control; they involve using goals that you set and train for.

Finally, allow appropriate time to attain your goals. Improvements in fitness level cannot occur overnight. As we discussed in chapter 4, it takes a minimum of four to six weeks to adapt the muscles that affect strength and performance. Flexibility, if done properly, also comes gradually through a dedicated program of static stretching. Typically, you should not retest your fitness levels sooner than eight weeks or, in many cases, every three months to allow adaptations and improvements in training to occur.

© Lance Jeffrey

PERIODIZATION TRAINING

Another important concept that we should discuss in dealing with fitness program design is *periodization*. Periodization is a long-term training plan that systematically controls and changes the volume, intensity, frequency, and duration of training and competition. Its purpose is to optimize performance at specific times and prevent overtraining, chronic fatigue, and burnout. The training volume relates to the amount of work you perform, the intensity refers to how hard you work in your training session, and the frequency measures how often you train. The duration relates to the length of your workout or training session.

Periodization has been used for many decades in sports such as weightlifting, swimming, and track and field, but it also has benefits for tennis players. Applying periodization to tennis allows a player to integrate many types of training in several specific time periods or stages. Each stage within a periodization cycle has a specific goal and purpose and allows the athlete to work toward competitive events in a structured way.

Have you ever noticed that tennis is one of the few sports without an off-season? If you want, you can play in a tournament every week. Sports such as basketball, baseball, and soccer have a specific time of the year when they compete and a time when the season ends. Although there can be advantages to playing in many events, the problem with playing tennis week after week is that you may risk injury, get stale, or even burn out.

What do many of our top professional players and USTA National Team members do to avoid these problems? They follow a carefully designed periodization training program. Each individualized periodization training program is based on your fitness level and your planned tournament schedule. Therefore, at the beginning of the year (with your coach if you have one) it is important to decide which tournaments are most important for your tennis development. Start by testing yourself using the USTA Fitness Testing Protocol (chapter 2) to determine your baseline fitness level, and then proceed with training. A tennis-specific periodization training program consists of four different phases: the preparation phase, the precompetitive phase, the competitive (peaking) phase, and the active rest (transition) phase.

Preparation Phase

It is important to develop a strong aerobic base in the preparation phase, focusing on high-volume and low-intensity work. This means that, in addition to your tennis practice, you should focus on long-distance activities such as running, biking, or swimming for at least 20 minutes continuously. The length of this phase may vary but should not be shorter than four weeks.

Preparation Phase

The training components of the preparation phase include the following:

- Challenge the aerobic energy system, for example, 20 to 40 minutes of aerobic training at 70 to 85 percent of maximum heart rate three to four times per week.
- Establish a strength base, for example, strength training using a high-repetition (10 to 15 repetitions per set, with 2 to 3 sets), low-resistance training program.
- Include technical and tactical training, for example on-court training that would incorporate changes in stroke mechanics, develop new shots, and so on.

There is little tennis-specific training in this phase. It emphasizes low resistance and high repetition to establish a fitness base. The later, more specific phases include lower work output and higher overall intensity.

Precompetitive Phase

In the precompetitive phase, training routines should become more tennis specific, increasing the intensity while reducing the training volume. Although there will still be an aerobic component to the training program, the focus should be more on explosive movement and strength-training exercises. Again, the length of this phase should be at least four weeks.

Precompetitive Phase

The second phase in the periodization cycle is termed the precompetitive phase. In this phase the intensity level increases and the theme becomes more tennis-specific.

- Challenge the anaerobic energy system, for example, on-court training drills, interval training using tennis-specific work:rest intervals.
- Improve speed and power, for example, sprinting and explosive on-court exercises, plyometrics.
- Improve muscular strength, for example, perform 2 to 4 sets with 8 to 10 repetitions, decrease the training volume, and increase the intensity of the resistance exercise.
- Maintain aerobic status, for example, perform aerobic exercise two times per week for 20 to 30 minutes.
- Improve tennis-specific skill, for example, on-court training focuses on tennis-specific drills, practice matches, and simulated points in preparation for competition.

Competitive (Peaking) Phase

Because athletes can sustain a true peak in performance for only three weeks, you should focus on maintaining strength and endurance levels during the competitive or peaking phase. Train at high intensities, while determining the volume by the number and length of matches and tournaments in this period. Players usually terminate aerobic training and weight training during this phase. Some athletes may travel with rubber tubing and perform a light set or two of 10 to 15 repetitions to maintain strength in tennis-specific areas, such as the rotator cuff or forearms, but the primary focus during this time remains on peak performance.

© Russ Adams Productions, Inc.

Peaking Phase

- Peak performance!
- High-intensity workouts.
- Tennis competition or tennis-specific training.

Active Rest

During the early part of active rest or transition phase, take some time to recover from tennis. Maintain your fitness level by participating in other activities, such as basketball, soccer, and running. As you start playing tennis again, work on your stroke technique. Depending on the time of year, this transition phase could last from one to four weeks. The goal in this phase is to rest from the physical and psychological stresses that training and competition apply.

Active Rest or Transition Phase

- Rest from tennis.
- Cross-train to maintain fitness levels.
- Emphasize fun, low-intensity workouts.
- Rest for one to four weeks.

ORGANIZING A PERIODIZED PROGRAM

Because most tennis players' schedules do not contain an off-season, applying the periodized model to tennis can be tricky. One way to structure the periodization cycle is to choose tournaments that carry the most significance, and build the training phases based on the performance peaks. For example, a player hoping to peak for the U.S. Open in late August would spend the four to six weeks before it in the precompetitive phase. The player would be in the preparation phase, with aerobic training, building a strength base, and so on, in early summer. An example of a periodized cycle is included in figure 8.1.

One complete periodization cycle is termed a microcycle, in which the athlete goes through each phase one time. Groupings of microcycles are

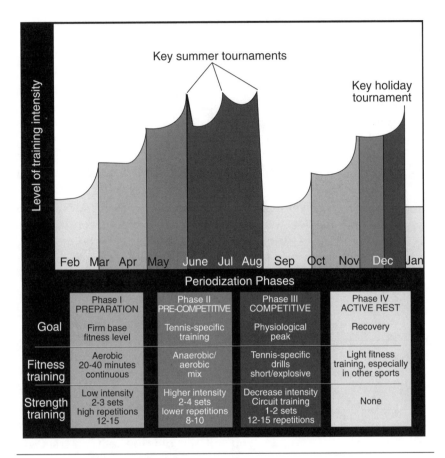

Figure 8.1   Sample periodized training cycle.
Reprinted, by permission, from Jack Groppel, USTA *Sport Science for Tennis Newsletter* Winter 1989, White Plains, NY: USTA, 1.

called a macrocycle, which often would contain an entire year's tournaments or performance schedule, as shown in figure 8.1. Following each microcycle of periodization, athletes typically do fitness testing and a needs analysis so the next training cycle can address specific weaknesses or injury risk characteristics and improve performance.

STARTING YOUR PROGRAM

Several principles may assist you in balancing the aspects of a training program and fitting them successfully into an effective regimen.

1. *Integrate flexibility training with all other aspects of your training.* There is not usually enough time for any athlete to spend an hour daily on stretching. However, if you integrate flexibility training before and after all other modes of training, then you usually won't require a specific block of time dedicated only to flexibility training. An example of how to incorporate flexibility with your tennis workouts is listed in chapter 3 (see table 3.1). Additionally, a brief stretching period before and after a weight workout or an aerobic training workout is as important and accomplishes the same goals as stretching before and after your on-court training.

2. *Prioritize!* A player who simultaneously implements several components—such as strength training, sprints, aerobic conditioning, and plyometrics—into a start-up fitness program is bound to fail. Pick one or two components to focus on initially, and build your program from that training focus to a more comprehensive program over time. An example would be adding a regimen of flexibility training before and after tennis play, along with shoulder and trunk exercises for two to four weeks. Then add items to the program, such as anaerobic, on-court drills or aerobic training. Begin with the one or two items that need the most emphasis, and build the program as your body allows.

3. *Don't expect immediate results.* If you do, you may be disappointed. As we discussed in the chapter on strength training (chapter 4), it takes a minimum of four to six weeks to change the muscle. Similarly, the program you initially develop may take several weeks to garner results—this is normal.

4. *More is not necessarily better. Remember to include rest and recovery.* When putting together a training program that includes several components, you cannot always perform every component every day. In many instances you can perform strength training two or three times per week, allowing the trained muscles to recover a day or two between sessions. The same would hold true for aerobic conditioning and other elements in the program.

In summary, we hope these principles will guide you in applying the individual concepts from the earlier chapters of this book. We present the sample workouts in the next chapter as templates for you to use and modify based on individual needs. Whether you're Pete Sampras, Anna Kournikova, an aspiring junior competitive player, or a recreational player, adding a fitness program will enhance your performance level and increase your enjoyment of the game.

CHAPTER 9

TENNIS-SPECIFIC CONDITIONING PROGRAMS

Each player has his or her specific strengths and weaknesses and can benefit from an individualized program. Throughout this book we have provided information on the necessary components of a total conditioning program: flexibility, aerobic and anaerobic conditioning, strength and power training, and on-court drills. The purpose of this chapter is to provide examples of tennis-specific conditioning programs to serve as templates, or skeletons, so you can design a program specifically geared for you. Many previous chapters have examples of exercises, drills, and workouts already, but here are a few additional ideas.

The training schedules and workout routines described in this chapter are examples of actual players' programs. Of course your own program will differ based on your fitness results (see chapter 2) and your tournament schedule. However, these programs can be used as a guideline to help you design your own individualized training schedule. As your season progresses, revisit your program occasionally to see if any modifications need to be made.

© Lance Jeffrey

PERIODIZING YOUR PROGRAM

Each periodization training program is based on your fitness level and your planned tournament schedule. Therefore, it is important to decide at the beginning of the year which tournaments are most important for your tennis career and development. In addition, you should determine your baseline fitness level (see chapter 2).

Preparation Phase

The goal is to build a strong aerobic base, emphasizing muscular and cardiorespiratory endurance. All forms of training should focus on high-volume, low-intensity work. In addition to your tennis training, you should do long-distance activities such as running, biking, or swimming for at least 20 minutes continuously. For strength training, use light weights with high repetitions across a wide range of exercises. The length of this phase will be approximately four weeks.

Precompetition Phase

The goal is to modify conditioning to simulate the demands of competitive tennis. Emphasize metabolic, movement, and muscle specificity, and focus training routines on strength and power, anaerobic endurance, and speed. In the beginning of this phase, there will still be an aerobic component to the training program, but as the peaking period or competition phase approaches, you will use smaller amounts of training at higher levels of intensity. Developing explosive power becomes more important toward the end of this phase. This phase will be approximately four weeks.

Competition Phase

The goal is to build optimum performance during the most important period of tournaments. Perform training at a high intensity; determine the volume by the number of matches or tournaments in the time period. Strength training during this time should be strictly for maintaining strength and power as well as anaerobic and muscular endurance. This phase will be two to three weeks.

Active Rest

This phase is also known as the transition phase. The goal of this period is to take some time away from the stresses of tennis. Maintain your fitness through playing other sports such as basketball or soccer. As you start playing tennis again, this is a good time to make any technique changes or modifications. Strength-training exercises should be low intensity and low volume. Depending on the time of year, this phase should last from one to four weeks.

Other Factors

Realize that these phases serve only as a guideline. The most important (and difficult) component of a proper periodization training program is when to give your body a rest. Many players will need to take a short break after two or three tough tournaments. Of course, much depends on how far you get in the tournament.

In addition, you should consider the following factors, which affect all players in different ways:

- Travel—international, time changes, nutrition and diet, sleep patterns
- Competition—intensity, seeding
- Practice and preparation—location, extended rest versus shorter but more frequent rest
- Court surfaces—adjustments of practice time
- Injuries—early intervention, proper medical care, time for rehabilitation
- Additional activities—social engagements, holidays, special events
- Team competition—high school or collegiate, league play, Fed Cup, Davis Cup, Olympics

PROFESSIONAL FEMALE PLAYER'S TRAINING SCHEDULE

Mary Joe Fernandez

Date	Location	Surface	Training notes
1/6	Sydney	Hard	Strength = 2-3x/wk Cardio = 1x/wk @ 80% max for 15 min; intervals 2x/wk Agility = 1-2x/wk
1/13	**Australian Open (Melbourne)**	**Hard**	Off—Just play tennis! Perform strength training only after conclusion of tournament.
1/27	Week off	Hard	Active rest
2/3	Week off	Hard	Strength = 3x/wk Cardio = 3x/wk @ 65% max for 30 min Agility = 1x/wk
2/10	Week off	Hard	Strength = 3x/wk Cardio = 2x/wk @ 65% max for 25 min; intervals 1x/wk; slide board 2x/wk for 2 min Agility = 2x/wk

2/17	Week off	Hard	Strength = 3x/wk Cardio = 2x/wk @ 70% max for 20 min; intervals 2x/wk; slide board 3x/wk for 4 min Agility = 3x/wk
2/24	Fed Cup	Hard	Strength = 3x/wk Cardio = 2x/wk @ 75% max for 15 min; intervals 1x/wk; slide board 2x/wk for 4 min Agility = 2-3x/wk
3/7	Indian Wells	Hard	Strength = 2-3x/wk Cardio = intervals 3x/wk; slide board 1x/wk for 5 min Agility = 1-2x/wk
3/17	**Lipton (Key Biscayne)**	**Hard**	Off—Just play tennis! Perform strength training only after conclusion of tournament.
3/31	Hilton Head	Clay	Strength = 2x/wk Cardio = 2x/wk @ 70% max for 20 min Agility = 2x/wk
4/7	Week off	Clay	Active rest
4/14	Week off	Clay	Strength = 3x/wk Cardio = 4x/wk @ 60% max for 25 min; slide board 1x/wk for 2 min Agility = none
4/21	Week off	Clay	Strength = 3x/wk Cardio = 3x/wk @ 65% max for 25 min; slide board 1x/wk for 2 min Agility = 1x/wk
5/1	Week off	Clay	Strength = 3x/wk Cardio = 3x/wk @ 70% max for 25 min; intervals 2x/wk; slide board 2x/wk for 2 min Agility = 2x/wk
5/7	Week off	Clay	Strength = 3x/wk Cardio = 1x/wk @ 75% max for 20 min; intervals 2x/wk; slide board 3x/wk for 4 min Agility = 3x/wk

Date	Tournament	Surface	Conditioning
5/14	Berlin	Clay	Strength = 2x/wk Cardio = 1x/wk @ 75% max for 20 min; intervals 1x/wk; slide board 2x/wk for 4 min Agility = 2x/wk
5/19	Madrid	Clay	Strength = 2x/wk Cardio = 1x/wk @ 80% max for 15 min; intervals 1x/wk; slide board 1x/wk for 5 min Agility = 1-2x/wk
5/26	**French Open (Roland Carros)**	**Clay**	Off—Just play tennis! Perform strength training only after conclusion of tournament.
6/5	Week off	Grass	1/2 week active rest Strength = 2x/wk Cardio = 2x/wk @ 65-70% max for 20 min; intervals 2x/wk; slide board 1x/wk for 3 min Agility = 1x/wk
6/16	Eastbourne	Grass	Strength = 2x/wk Cardio = intervals 3x/wk Agility = 1-2x/wk
6/23	**Wimbledon**	**Grass**	Off—Just play tennis! Perform strength training only after conclusion of tournament.
7/7	Fed Cup	TBD	Strength = 2-3x/wk Cardio = 2x/wk @ 60% max for 30 min Agility = 1x/wk
7/10	Week off	Hard	Strength = 3x/wk Cardio = 3x/wk @ 70% max for 25 min; intervals 1x/wk Agility = 3x/wk
7/21	Stanford	Hard	Strength = 2-3x/wk Cardio = 2x/wk @ 75% max for 20 min; intervals 1x/wk Agility = 2x/wk
7/26	Week off	Hard	Strength = 3x/wk Cardio = 2x/wk @ 75% max for 20 min; intervals 3x/wk Agility = 3x/wk

8/4	Week off	Hard	Strength = 3x/wk Cardio = 2x/wk @ 80% max for 15 min; intervals 3x/wk Agility = 3x/wk
8/11	Toronto	Hard	Strength = 2x/wk Cardio = 1x/wk @ 75% max for 15 min; intervals 2x/wk Agility = 2x/wk
8/18	Week off	Hard	Strength = 3x/wk Cardio = intervals 3x/wk Agility = 1-2x/wk
8/25	**U.S. Open (Flushing Meadow)**	**Hard**	Off—Just play tennis! Perform strength training only after conclusion of tournament.
9/3	Week off	Hard	Active rest
9/10	Week off	Hard	Strength = 3x/wk Cardio = 2x/wk @ 65% max for 25 min; intervals 1x/wk Agility = 1-2x/wk
9/20	Week off	Hard	Strength = 3x/wk Cardio = 2x/wk @ 75% max for 15 min; intervals 1x/wk Agility = 2x/wk
9/29	Fed Cup	TBD	Strength = 2-3x/wk Cardio = 1x/wk @ 75% max for 20 min Agility = 1-2x/wk
10/6	Filderstadt	Indoor Supreme	Strength = 2-3x/wk Cardio = 2x/wk @ 70% max for 25 min; intervals 1x/wk Agility = 2x/wk
10/13	Zurich	Indoor Supreme	Strength = 2-3x/wk Cardio = 1x/wk @ 65% max for 30 min; intervals 2x/wk Agility = 2x/wk
10/20	Week off	Hard	Strength = 3x/wk Cardio = 2x/wk @ 75% max for 20 min; intervals 2x/wk Agility = 3x/wk

10/27	Week off	Hard	Strength = 3x/wk Cardio 2x/wk @ 80% max for 15 min; intervals 1x/wk Agility = 2-3x/wk
11/3	Chicago	Hard	Strength = 2-3x/wk Cardio = 1x/wk @ 80% max for 10-15 min; intervals 2x/wk Agility = 2x/wk
11/10	Week off	Hard	Strength = 2-3x/wk Cardio = intervals 3x/wk Agility = 1-2x/wk
11/17	**New York**	**Indoor Supreme**	Off—Just play tennis! Perform strength training only after conclusion of tournament.
11/23	Week off	Hard	Active rest
12/1	Week off	Hard	Strength = 4x/wk Cardio = 2x/wk @ 65% max for 25 min; intervals 2x/wk; slide board 2x/wk for 2 min Agility = 2x/wk
12/7	Week off	Hard	Strength = 4x/wk Cardio = 4x/wk @ 70% for 25 min; intervals 2x/wk; slide board 3x/wk for 4 min Agility = 3x/wk
12/14	Week off	Hard	Strength = 4x/wk Cardio = 4x/wk @ 75% for 25 min; intervals 2x/wk; slide board 4x/wk for 5 min Agility = 3x/wk
12/21	Week off	Hard	Strength = 4x/wk Cardio = 3x/wk @ 75% for 20 min; intervals 3x/wk; slide board 2x/wk for 5 min Agility = 2-3x/wk

Note:
- Each recorded date relates to that week or tournament.
- Highlighted areas signify peak performance periods.
- % max estimates are based on (a) the athlete's perceived exertion during exercise, or (b) heart rate calculations, as presented in chapter 5: $THR(60\%) = (220 - Age)0.60$

Example: THR(60%) = (220 − 26 years old)0.60 = 116 bpm

This range lets the athlete monitor intensity throughout the exercise bout, thus allowing optimal performance enhancement.

Guidelines

1. Preparation period.
   - Low intensity, high volume, low specificity of training.
   - Three or four sets of 12 to 15 repetitions. Focus on increasing endurance.
2. Precompetition and competition period.
   - High intensity, low volume, high specificity of training.
   - Three sets of 8 to 10 repetitions (about 1-2 weeks before projected peak performance). Focus on increasing strength and power.
3. Cardiovascular training.
   - Distance running—15 to 30 minutes at a desired intensity level, and/or
   - Interval training—ten to fifteen 20-yard sprints with 12 to 20 seconds rest between bouts. Emphasize maximum power on first step. Perform on grass or slightly cushioned surface if possible.
4. Agility training—plyometrics or tennis-specific movement training. Perform on grass or slightly cushioned surface if possible.
5. Flexibility training must be performed every day.

PROFESSIONAL MALE PLAYER'S TRAINING SCHEDULE

David DiLucia

Date	Location	Surface	Training notes
12/29	Week off	Hard	Strength = 3x/wk Cardio = 2-3x/wk @ 80% max for 15 min; Agility = 3x/wk
1/5	Adelaide	Hard	Strength = 2-3x/wk Cardio = 2x/wk @ 80% max for 15 min; intervals 4-5x/wk; Agility = 2x/wk

1/12	Auckland	Hard	Strength = 2-3x/wk Cardio = 1x/wk @ 85% max for 10 min; intervals 3-4x/wk; Agility = 1-2x/wk
1/19	**Australian Open (Melbourne)**	**Hard**	Off—Just play tennis! Only train after conclusion of tournament. Strength = 1-2x/wk (*maintenance*) Cardio = 1x/wk @ 75% max for 20 min; intervals 1-2x/wk; Agility = 1-2x/wk
1/26	**Australian Open (Melbourne)**	**Hard**	Off—Just play tennis! Only train after conclusion of tournament. Strength = 1-2x/wk (*maintenance*) Cardio = 2x/wk @ 70% max for 20 min; intervals 1-2x/wk; slide board 1-2x/wk for 2 min Agility = 1-2x/wk (1/2 Active rest if possible)
2/2	West Bloomfield, Michigan	Hard	Strength = 2-3x/wk Cardio = 2x/wk @ 75% max for 20 min; intervals 4x/wk; slide board 2x/wk for 3 min Agility = 2-3x/wk
2/9	San Jose	Hard	Strength = 2-3x/wk Cardio = 2x/wk @ 75% max for 20 min; intervals 3x/wk; slide board 3x/wk for 3 min Agility = 3x/wk
2/16	Week off	Hard	Strength = 3x/wk Cardio = 2x/wk @ 80% max for 15 min; intervals 4-5x/wk; slide board 2x/wk for 3 min Agility = 3x/wk
2/23	Philadelphia	Hard	Strength = 2-3x/wk Cardio = 1x/wk @ 80% max for 10 min; intervals 4x/wk; slide board 1x/wk (15 x 10 sec) Agility = 2-3x/wk
3/2	Week off	Hard	Strength = 2-3x/wk Cardio = 3x/wk @ 60% max for 25 min; intervals 4x/wk; slide board 1x/wk (10 x 10 sec) Agility = 2-3x/wk

3/9	Salinas	Hard	Strength = 2-3x/wk Cardio = 1x/wk @ 80% max for 15 min; intervals 3x/wk Agility = 1-2x/wk
3/16	**Lipton (Key Biscayne)**	**Hard**	Off—Just play tennis! Only train after conclusion of tournament. Strength = 1-2x/wk (*maintenance*) Cardio = 1x/wk @ 75% max for 20 min; intervals 2x/wk; Agility = 1-2x/wk
3/23	**Lipton (Key Biscayne)**	**Hard**	Off—Just play tennis! Active rest after conclusion of tournament
3/30	Week off	Hard	(1/2 Active rest only if played 2nd week of Lipton) Strength = 2-3x/wk Cardio = 2x/wk @ 70% max for 25 min; intervals 2x/wk; slide board 1-2x/wk for 2 min Agility = 2x/wk
4/6	Chennai	Hard	Strength = 2-3x/wk Cardio = 2x/wk @ 75% max for 25 min; intervals 3x/wk; slide board 3x/wk for 3 min Agility = 3x/wk
4/13	Tokyo	Hard	Strength = 2-3x/wk Cardio = 2-3x/wk @ 75% max for 25 min; intervals 3x/wk; slide board 3x/wk for 5 min Agility = 2x/wk
4/20	Espinho	Clay	Strength = 2-3x/wk Cardio = 2-3x/wk @ 75% max for 25 min; intervals 3x/wk; slide board 3x/wk for 5 min Agility = 3x/wk
4/27	Munich	Clay	Strength = 2-3x/wk Cardio = 2-3x/wk @ 75% max for 20 min; intervals 3x/wk; slide board 3x/wk for 4 min Agility = 2x/wk
5/4	Ljubljana	Clay	Strength = 2-3x/wk Cardio = 2-3x/wk @ 75% max for 20 min; intervals 3x/wk; slide board 2-3x/wk for 2 min Agility = 3x/wk

5/11	Rome	Clay	Strength = 2x/wk Cardio = 2-3x/wk @ 80% max for 15 min; intervals 3x/wk; slide board 2x/wk (15 x 20 sec) Agility = 2x/wk
5/18	Week off	Clay	Strength = 2-3x/wk Cardio = 2x/wk @ 80% max for 15 min; intervals 2-3x/wk; slide board 2x/wk (10 x 10 sec) Agility = 1-2x/wk
5/25	**French Open (Roland Garros)**	**Clay**	Off—Just play tennis! Train only after conclusion of tournament. Strength = 1-2x/wk (*maintenance*) Cardio = 1-2x/wk @ 70% max for 20 min; intervals 1-2x/wk Agility = 1-2x/wk
6/1	**French Open (Roland Garros)**	**Clay**	Off—Just play tennis! Train only after conclusion of tournament. Strength = 1-2x/wk (*maintenance*) Cardio = 1-2x/wk @ 75% max for 15 min; intervals 3x/wk Agility = 1-2x/wk
6/8	Queens	Grass	Strength = 1-2x/wk Cardio = 2x/wk @ 80% max for 15 min; intervals 4x/wk; slide board 2x/wk (5 x 15 sec) Agility = 1-2x/wk
6/15	Week off	Grass	Strength = 2x/wk Cardio = intervals 4-5x/wk; slide board 2-3x/wk (10 x 10 sec) Agility = 2-3x/wk
6/22	**Wimbledon**	**Grass**	Off—Just play tennis! Only train after conclusion of tournament. Strength = 1-2x/wk (*maintenance*) Cardio = 1-2x/wk @ 85% max for 10 min Agility = 1-2x/wk
6/29	**Wimbledon**	**Grass**	Off—Just play tennis! Only train after conclusion of tournament. Strength = 2x/wk (*maintenance*) Cardio = 1-2x/wk @ 85% max for 10 min Agility = 1-2x/wk

7/6	Newport/ Team Tennis	Grass	Strength = 2x/wk Cardio = 1x/wk @ 75% max for 20 min; intervals 2x/wk Agility = 1-2x/wk
7/13	Team Tennis	Hard	1/2 Active rest Strength = 2x/wk Cardio = 2-3x/wk @ 70% max for 20 min; intervals 1x/wk Agility = 2x/wk
7/20	Washington/ Team Tennis	Hard	Strength = 3x/wk Cardio = 2x/wk @ 75% max for 20 min; intervals 3x/wk Agility = 2-3x/wk
7/27	Los Angeles	Hard	Strength = 3x/wk Cardio = 2x/wk @ 75% max for 20 min; intervals 3x/wk Agility = 3x/wk
8/3	Toronto	Hard	Strength = 3x/wk Cardio = 1x/wk @ 80% max for 15 min; intervals 2x/wk Agility = 3-4x/wk
8/10	Cincinnati	Hard	Strength = 3x/wk Cardio = 1x/wk @ 80% max for 10 min; intervals 3-4x/wk Agility = 3-4x/wk
8/17	Indianapolis	Hard	Strength = 3x/wk Cardio = intervals 3-4x/wk Agility = 2-3x/wk
8/24	Long Island	Hard	Strength = 2x/wk Cardio = intervals 3x/wk Agility = 2x/wk
8/31	**U.S. Open (Flushing Meadow)**	**Hard**	Off—Just play tennis! Active rest after conclusion of tournament.
9/7	**U.S. Open (Flushing Meadow)**	**Hard**	Off—Just play tennis! Active rest after conclusion of tournament.
9/14	Team Tennis	Hard	(Only active rest if lost late in U.S. Open) Strength = 2x/wk Cardio = 2x/wk @ 65% max for 20 min Agility = 1x/wk

9/21	Team Tennis	Hard	Strength = 3x/wk Cardio = 2x/wk @ 70% max for 20 min; intervals 1x/wk Agility = 1-2x/wk

Suggested Schedule

Monday-Wednesday-Friday
1. Weight training
2. Cardiovascular training on bike

Tuesday-Thursday
1. Sprint training
   - 5-10 repetitions
   - Rest while walking to start position
2. Jump rope
   - 5-10 minutes nonstop
   - Count number of touches (minimum 250 touches)
3. Ladder drills:
   - Run through touching each box once, every other box, every third box, and so on until full stride length is attained
   - Knee high kicks
   - Heel kicks
   - Carioca
   - Double leg hops in each box—progress to three up, one back
   - Single leg hops in each box (front, lateral, medial hopping)—progress to three up, one back
   - Lateral jumps (hold each landing for one second) (skiing)
   - Side-to-side in and out of each box ("Icky shuffle")

Note: Always stretch after each workout!

FEMALE COLLEGIATE PLAYER'S TRAINING SCHEDULE

Date	Location	Training notes
5/28-31	Week off	Strength = evaluation; 2x/wk (2 sets x 12 reps) Cardio = testing/evaluation; 1x/wk @ 90% max for 12 min; Agility = testing/evaluation; 1x/wk
6/1-7	Week off	Strength = 3x/wk (2 sets x 12 reps) Cardio = 3x/wk @ 65% max for 25 min; intervals 2x/wk; slide board 2x/wk for 3 min Agility = 2x/wk
6/8-14	Week off	Strength = 3x/wk (3 sets x 12 reps) Cardio = 4x/wk @ 70% max for 25 min; intervals 1x/wk; slide board 3x/wk for 3 min Agility = 3x/wk
6/15-21	Week off	Strength = 3x/wk (4 sets x 15 reps) Cardio = 5x/wk @ 75% max for 20 min; intervals 1x/wk; slide board 2x/wk for 4 min Agility = 3x/wk
6/22-28	Week off	Strength = 3x/wk (4 sets x 15 reps) Cardio = 4x/wk @ 75% max for 20 min; intervals 1x/wk; slide board 2x/wk for 3 min Agility = 3x/wk
6/29-7/5	Week off	Strength = 3x/wk (3 sets x 12 reps) Cardio = 2x/wk @ 80% max for 15 min; intervals 2x/wk; slide board 1x/wk for 2 min Agility = 2-3x/wk
7/6-8/2	Summer tournament circuit (1 clay/ 3 hard)	Strength = 2x/wk (maintenance) Cardio = 1x/wk @ 65% max for 20 min; intervals 2-3x/wk (depending on match load played/wk) Agility = 1-2x/wk (on light match days only)
8/3-9	Week off	Strength = 3x/wk (3 sets x 15 reps) Cardio = 2x/wk @ 55-60% max for 30 min; intervals 1x/wk Agility = 1x/wk
8/10-16	Week off	Strength = 3x/wk (3 sets x 15 reps) Cardio = 4x/wk @ 70% max for 20 min; intervals 2x/wk Agility = 2x/wk

8/17-23	Tennis team	Strength = 3x/wk (4 sets x 12 reps) Cardio = 2x/wk @ 75% max for 20 min; intervals 1x/wk Agility = 3x/wk
8/24-30	Tennis team	Strength = 3x/wk (4 sets x 12 reps) Cardio = 3x/wk @ 75% max for 20 min; intervals 1x/wk Agility = 3x/wk
8/31-9/6	Tennis team	Strength = 3x/wk (3 sets x 8-10 reps) Cardio = 1x/wk @ 75% max for 25 min; intervals 3x/wk Agility = 3x/wk
9/7-13	Tennis team	Strength = 3x/wk (3 sets x 8-10 reps) Cardio = 2x/wk @ 75% max for 30 min; intervals 2x/wk Agility = 3x/wk
9/14-20	Tennis team	Strength = 3x/wk (3 sets x 15 reps) Cardio = 3x/wk @ 75% max for 25 min; intervals 2x/wk Agility = 3x/wk
9/21-27	Tennis team	Strength = 3x/wk (3 sets x 15 reps) Cardio = 4x/wk @ 75% max for 20 min Agility = 3x/wk
9/28-10/4	Tennis team	Strength = evaluation; 3x/wk (3 sets x 12 reps) Cardio = testing/evaluation; 1x/wk @ 90% max for 12 min; intervals 1x/wk; slide board 1x/wk for 2 min Agility = testing/evaluation; 2x/wk

Guidelines

1. Preparation period.
   - Low intensity, high volume, low specificity.
   - Three or four sets of 12 to 15 repetitions.
2. Precompetition and competition period.
   - High intensity, low volume, high specificity.
   - Three sets of 8 to 10 repetitions (about one to two weeks before projected peak performance).
   - Use at your discretion through trial and error.

3. Cardiovascular training.

- Distance running—15 to 30 minutes at a particular intensity level, and/or

- Interval training—ten to fifteen 20-yard sprints with 12 to 20 seconds rest between bouts. Emphasize maximum power on first step.

4. Flexibility training must be performed every day.

NATIONALLY RANKED JUNIOR PLAYER'S TRAINING SCHEDULE

One Month Training Program

Surface	Date	Event	Location	Training notes
Hard	5/7-9	State H.S. champ	Orlando	Strength = 2x/wk (3 sets x 8-10 reps) Cardio = 2x/wk @ 65% max for 20 min
Clay	5/16-21	USTA 1st qualifying	Deerfield Beach	Strength = 3x/wk (3 sets x 8-10 reps) Cardio = 1x/wk @ 75% max for 15 min; intervals 2x/wk
Clay	**5/24-26**	**Sectional Tournament**	**Delray Beach**	Off—Just play tennis!
Clay	5/31-6/4	USTA 3rd qualifying	Tampa	Strength = 3x/wk (3 sets x 8-10 reps) Cardio = 3x/wk @ 70% max for 20 min
Hard	6/7-9	Tune-Up Tourney		Strength = 3x/wk (3 sets x 8-10 reps) Cardio = 1x/wk @ 80% max for 15 min; intervals 2x/wk
Hard	**6/14-19**	**FL State champ.**		Off—Do not perform strength training until the conclusion of tournament play.

Guidelines

1. Preparation period.
   - Low intensity, high volume, low specificity.
   - Three or four sets of 8 to 12 repetitions.
2. Precompetition and competition period.
   - High intensity, low volume, high specificity.
   - Three sets of 8 to 10 repetitions (about one to two weeks before projected peak performance).
3. Cardiovascular training.
   - Distance running—15 to 30 minutes at a particular intensity level, and/or
   - Interval training—ten to fifteen 20-yard sprints with 12 to 20 seconds rest between bouts. Emphasize maximum power on first step.
4. Flexibility training must be performed every day.

AVID ADULT PLAYER'S TRAINING SCHEDULE

Surface	Date	Event	Training notes
Hard	6/4-7	Club tournament	Strength = 2-3x/wk (3 sets x 15 reps) Cardio = 2-3x/wk @ 60% max for 20 min; intervals 1x/wk
Hard	6/18-21	Local tournament	Strength = 2-3x/wk (3 sets x 12 reps) Cardio = 1x/wk @ 65% max for 20 min; intervals 1x/wk
Hard	7/9-12	Local tournament	Strength = 2-3x/wk (3 sets x 10 reps) Cardio = 1x/wk @ 70% max for 20 min; intervals 1x/wk
Hard	**7/23-26**	**City championship**	Off—Just play tennis!
Hard	8/6-9	Sectional tournament	Strength = 2-3x/wk (3 sets x 10 reps) Cardio = 2x/wk @ 70% max for 20 min; intervals 2x/wk

Hard	8/20-23	Sectional championship	Off—Just play tennis!
Clay (if possible)	8/24-9/6	Weeks off	Active rest—light tennis, strength training, swim, bike, run Strength = 3x/wk (3 sets x 12 reps) Cardio = 3x/wk @ 60% max for 30 min; no intervals
Hard or clay	9/7-...	USTA league	Resume normal, active tennis schedule. Strength = 3x/wk (3 sets x 15, 12, 10, or 8 reps) Cardio = 2-3x/wk @ 65-70% max for 20-30 min; intervals 1x/wk

Notes:
Bold print designates peak tournaments.
Weeks not mentioned should include:

- tennis,
- minimum of 2-3 days of cardiovascular training (bike, swin, run, etc.), and
- minimum of 2-3 days of resistance training (strength) with the same sets x repetitions according to the previously scheduled week.

Guidelines

1. Cardiovascular training.

- Distance running—20 to 30 minutes relative to a particular intensity level, and/or

- Interval training—one or two sets of five sprints per set (5-10 total), 20-yard sprints with 12 to 20 seconds rest between bouts. Emphasize maximum power on first step.

2. Flexibility training must be performed every day.

YOUR TRAINING SCHEDULE

Surface	Date	Event	Training notes
			Strength =
			Cardio =
			Agility =
			Strength =
			Cardio =
			Agility =
			Strength =
			Cardio =
			Agility =
			Strength =
			Cardio =
			Agility =
			Strength =
			Cardio =
			Agility =
			Strength =
			Cardio =
			Agility =

Strength =

Cardio =

Agility =

Strength =

Cardio =

Agility =

Strength =

Cardio =

Agility =

Strength =

Cardio =

Agility =

Strength =

Cardio =

Agility =

Strength =

Cardio =

Agility =

Strength =

Cardio =

Agility =

SAMPLE TENNIS-SPECIFIC WORKOUTS

WEIGHT-ROOM WORKOUT

Warm-Up
- Three to five minutes jumping rope, biking, and so on.
- Perform light stretching.

Body part	Exercise	Sets x reps
Chest	Dumbbell press	3 x 12
Back	Row	3 x 12
Shoulder (kneeling, arm 90 degrees abducted)	External rotation	3 x 12
	Prone horizontal abduction	3 x 12
Legs	Lunges	3 x 12
Biceps	Curls	3 x 12
Triceps	Extensions	3 x 12
Shoulder (standing, upper arm parallel to body)	External rotation (w/tubing)	3 x 12
Legs	Leg extension	3 x 12
Low back	Superman	1-3 sets
Abs	Crunches	1-3 sets
Flexibility	Stretch	20 minutes

MEDICINE BALL WORKOUT

1. Mini-tennis versus opponent—use both forehand and backhand sides.
2. Medicine ball sit-up.
   - Your partner throws the ball at chest level or just above your head.
   - You catch the ball while lowering yourself to the ground and throw the ball while returning to the sit-up position.
3. Receive, twist, throw.
   - Your partner throws the medicine ball to you.
   - After receiving the ball and twisting twice to each side, throw the ball to your partner.
   - Repeat this exercise on the other side.
4. Plyometric sit-up.
   - Your partner stands above you and pushes your legs toward the floor.
   - Prevent your feet from touching the floor and return to start position.
5. Crunches, twists, and leg raises.
   - One set is when you complete all three movements.
   - Perform 10, 15, or 20 repetitions of each movement.

CIRCUIT-TRAINING WORKOUT

Stations	Description
1. Push-ups	Elbow should be flexed 90 degrees at down position.
2. Crunches	Hands are across chest; upper back (shoulder blades) should come up and off the ground. Touch elbows to knees; hold medicine ball behind head for increased resistance.

3.	Oblique twists	Lying on back, try to touch shoulder to knees. It's impossible, but if elbows are to knees, you have not enough rotation. In a seated position, hold medicine ball at waist and twist side to side, trying to touch the ball to ground behind lower back.
4.	Superman	Lift arm and leg (opposite sides of both) and hold for 1 second before lowering.
5.	Ladder drills	Move through length of ladder and back for entire time; see chapter for drills. Be creative!
6.	Lunges	Use body weight or medicine ball behind head for resistance. Keep chest out and lower back tight; knees should not pass beyond toes.
7.	Right and left internal rotation	Attach tubing/band to stationary object (pole). Perform inward motion toward chest; keep elbow at side. See chapter 4.
8.	Right and left external rotation	Attach tubing/band to stationary object (pole). Perform outward rotation away from chest; keep elbow at side. See chapter 4.
9.	Seated row	Attach band to stationary object (pole). In seated position perform rowing motion; try to squeeze shoulder blades together.
10.	Jump rope	Medium to fast pace; concentrate on no misses (rhythm)!

Training Notes

- Focus on high volume (i.e., at least 12-15 repetitions per set) and low intensity. Build a base for the future!

- Frequency should be two or three workouts per week (three out of season, two or three in season). Use a logical progression, starting with one workout per week and proceeding to two or three times per week after you have adapted (absence of soreness or tightness).

- Perform workouts every other day (24 hours between workouts).

- Your time limit can be 15 to 20 *workout seconds* per station; you should attain at least 12 to 15 repetitions within this time limit. Proceed one to three times through the circuit.

- Always stretch before and after each workout. The post-workout stretch should be more comprehensive than the pre-workout stretch because enhanced flexibility, not warming up, is the key.

- Use caution when you are performing plyometrics. Most plyometrics are advanced jumping or hopping exercises that increase your maximal power output and, therefore, require a good strength base. Make sure your knees do not collapse inward during plyometrics. This will usually occur with beginners and is a major determinant of physical ability or inability to perform plyometric exercises.

- Perform plyometrics in your circuit only one or two times per week (once at the onset of your circuit routine). Omit the ladder and jump rope stations.

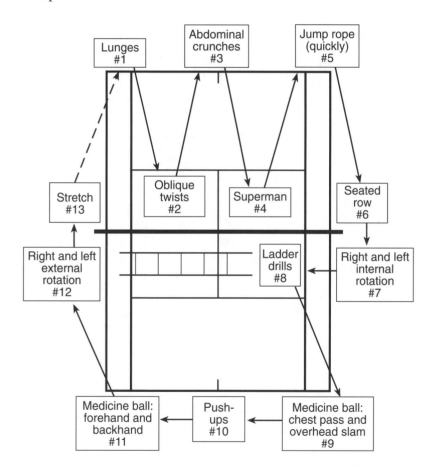

MOVEMENT CIRCUIT TRAINING

Note: Precede your on-court workout with a warm-up (light jog or jump rope).

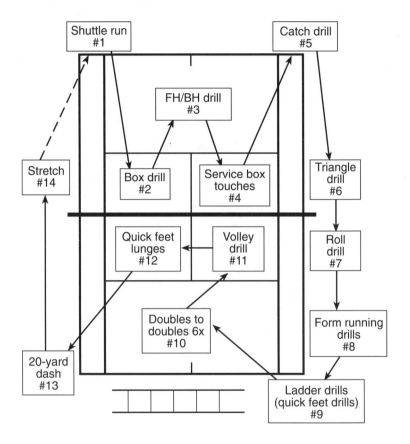

PLYOMETRIC CIRCUIT TRAINING

Note: Precede your on-court workout with a warm-up (light jog or jump rope).

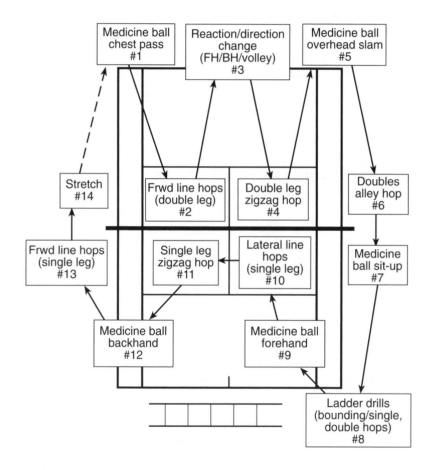

OBSTACLE COURSE GAME

- Set up any four to six stations that go quickly, with 10 repetitions per station if applicable.
- Each player goes through the stations at 10 repetitions per station and touches the next player when finished.
- Divide players into two teams.
- The first team through the obstacle course wins (i.e., gets to choose the activity for the next practice day).

CIRCUIT WORKOUT

- Set up the 10 stations listed previously and rotate every 15 to 20 seconds; players may need to cover some stations more than once if they involve both right and left sides.
- Vary the order of stations between each workout to prevent staleness.
- Be creative with the set-up of your stations, especially if you have limited time and equipment.

CHAPTER 10

INJURY-FREE TENNIS

Many of us watched with horror

Boris Becker's forehand service return in the 1996 Wimbledon and were shocked at the extent of the injury to his wrist following that one shot. When interviewed after the match, Boris stated that he hit that forehand service return the same way he had hit it thousands and thousands of times before. Boris was correct in analyzing his wrist injury, and his analysis holds true for most injuries in tennis players.

INJURY TERMS

Injuries in tennis players are typically *overuse* injuries. An overuse injury results from repetitive stresses and minor traumatic events, such as the effects on the shoulder of serving thousands of times or the influence on the knees of playing hundreds of points with pivots, twists, and aggressive stops and starts. Overuse injuries occur because tennis players exert and produce forces in a repetitive pattern, accumulating minor traumas that cause tissue breakdown.

One unique thing about tennis is that it stresses nearly all areas of the body. The demands of tennis can be demonstrated by analyzing injury locations of top U.S. junior players (see figure 10.1). You can see that, although more injuries occurred to the shoulder, back, knees, and elbow, nearly all joints were affected by the demands of this great game. The shoulder was the number one area of complaint among players at the U.S. Open Tennis Championships in 1995.

Tennis injuries fall into two categories: acute and chronic. *Acute injury* describes a new injury or complaint from the time it occurs and the short time following the start of the injury. An example of an acute injury suffered by many tennis players would be an ankle sprain. A *chronic injury* typically recurs or repeats itself due to continued tennis play or

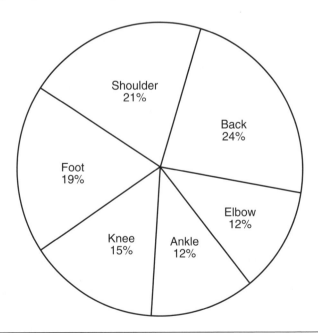

Figure 10.1 Injury breakdown of elite Junior Tennis players. (Percentages do not add to 100 due to rounding.)

lack of proper rehabilitation. An example of a chronic tennis injury would be tennis elbow that has been present for one or two years and flares up during long, grueling tournaments. Acute injuries in tennis are much easier to take care of, and when you address them initially, you can prevent the acute injury from becoming chronic.

PREVENTING INJURIES

How do you prevent a tennis injury from occurring? Although this may seem like a simple, straightforward question, the answer is complex. That is why we have written the preceding nine chapters in this book. You guessed it: the best way to prevent an injury is to condition yourself optimally for tennis and prepare your body for the stresses of the game.

In years past, many health professionals and tennis coaches said, "Play tennis to get in shape." Although an admirable reason to play tennis, due to its benefits on the heart and lungs, muscles and bones, that statement doesn't reflect the current thinking and overlying theme of this book. The key to preventing injuries and optimizing performance in tennis is clearly, "Get in shape to play tennis."

The most important concepts for injury prevention are also important for performance enhancement. These concepts are flexibility, strength training, aerobic and anaerobic training, and proper sport biomechanics. Tennis players can use the strategies in this chapter to prevent injury in these commonly stressed areas: the shoulder, trunk and low back, elbow, arm, and knee. Strength and flexibility exercises, as well as proper biomechanics, form the foundation of an injury-prevention program.

SHOULDER INJURIES

Overuse injury to the shoulder in tennis is common, ranging from the elite junior player to the senior recreational player. The shoulder is one of the most mobile joints in the human body, and, because of its large range of motion, can become injured during tennis play. The shoulder, or glenohumeral joint, consists of a ball (humerus) and socket (glenoid), without the benefit of a deep socket like that found in the human hip joint (see figure 10.2). Therefore, the muscles and ligaments surrounding the shoulder must work hard to maintain the ball in the socket, especially during the rapid movements in tennis, which occur as fast as 2500 degrees per second. (That's similar to the rotation of the wheels on

Managing Tennis Injuries: PRICE Method

Protect
Rest
Ice
Compress
Elevate

This handy saying summarizes many concepts in dealing with an acute tennis injury. *Protect* means to protect the injured area from further stress. It doesn't mean that you must place every injury in a cast or keep it from moving at all, but that you should minimize or remove the stresses that caused the injury.

Rest implies that you should rest the area to allow healing and prevent further injury. *Ice* indicates applying ice to the injured area, which will minimize swelling and decrease pain and inflammation. Typically, you can apply ice for 10 to 20 minutes, which constricts (narrows) the blood vessels in that area. Application of ice continues after an injury for several days with no time limitation (e.g., 48 or 72 hours). A decrease in pain and swelling are better indicators that you can discontinue icing than a rigid time period.

Compression assists, along with ice, by preventing swelling. Typically, players use an elastic bandage and wrap it around the injured area. The compression wrap also provides support to the injured area. *Elevate* applies mainly to injury to the knee, ankle, and foot or the elbow, wrist, and hand and instructs us to elevate the injured area relative to the heart. This helps prevent swelling or pooling of fluids in the injured area and uses gravity to decrease the swelling already present.

With all tennis injuries, the initial safe step is to apply the principles of PRICE. We always recommend that a medical professional evaluate your injury, whether it's a first-time ankle sprain or a chronic problem with your shoulder.

a bike traveling 32 miles per hour or 417 times faster than the rotation of the second hand on a clock!)

The primary muscles that hold the ball in the socket are the rotator cuff muscles (see figure 10.3). These four muscles originate back on your shoulder blade and insert in the shoulder, forming a cuff around the ball (humerus). Biomechanical research tells us that the rotator cuff is active

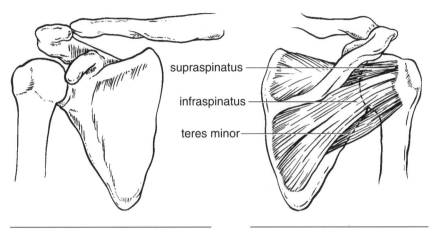

Figure 10.2   Shoulder joint.   **Figure 10.3**   Rotator cuff muscles.

during all tennis strokes. It accelerates the arm forward during the serve and slows the arm down after ball impact and during follow-through.

One common shoulder injury is a damaged rotator cuff resulting from its repetitive muscle work. The tendon is the structure that attaches the muscle to bone, and in the rotator cuff, it becomes inflamed from the heavy workloads of the tennis strokes. In general, tendons heal slowly, because their blood supply and healing potential is less than muscle.

One factor that makes the tennis player vulnerable to an overuse shoulder injury is muscle imbalance. Typically the anterior (front) muscles of the shoulder and chest, such as the pectorals and anterior deltoids, are much stronger than the rotator cuff and upper back muscles that support the shoulder blades (scapula). Research using isokinetic Cybex equipment on elite junior and adult tennis players confirms this muscle imbalance, and provides rationale for using tennis-specific strengthening exercises to prevent rotator cuff injury.

Strength Exercises to Prevent Shoulder Injury

The rotator cuff exercises in chapter 4 offer preventative conditioning for the tennis player. We recommend using a low-resistance, high-repetition format (e.g., 3 sets of 15 repetitions) with a light weight (as little as one or two pounds, progressing over time based on your strength to a maximum of four or five pounds). We do not recommend using heavier weights (greater than five pounds), because it will force the body to use larger muscle groups, such as the trapezius and deltoid.

Another common mistake is lifting weights overhead (higher than the shoulders). As we mentioned earlier, the shoulder is seldom lifted overhead in tennis strokes, even on the serve, hence the safer position to specifically train the rotator cuff muscles is using the patterns in the exercises that follow. Complete descriptions of the following rotator cuff exercises can be found on the page numbers in parentheses.

- Prone horizontal abduction (p. 85)
- 90-90 external rotation (p. 86)
- Scaption (empty can) (p. 87)
- External shoulder rotation with rubber tubing (p. 88)
- Internal shoulder rotation with rubber tubing (p. 89)
- External shoulder rotation with abduction (p. 89)

The following exercises will also strengthen your rotator cuff muscles.

SIDE-LYING EXTERNAL ROTATION

Starting Position: Lie on your side, with the opposite arm at your side and a small pillow between your arm and body.

Exercise Action: Keeping your elbow bent and fixed to your side, raise the arm into external rotation. Slowly lower to starting position and repeat.

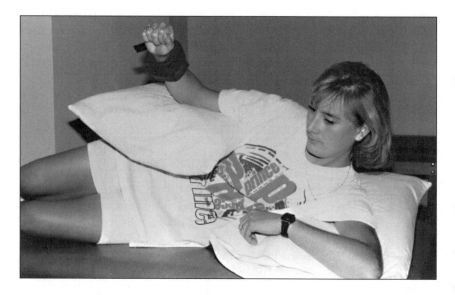

SHOULDER EXTENSION

Starting Position: Lie on a table on your stomach with your arm hanging straight to the floor.

Exercise Action: With your thumb pointed forward, raise your arm straight back into extension toward your hip. Slowly lower your arm and repeat.

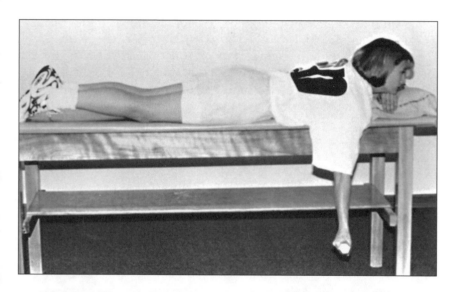

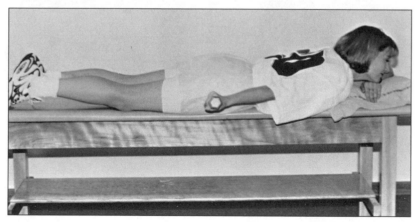

Scapular Stabilizing Exercises

In addition to working the rotator cuff muscles to balance strength in the tennis player's shoulder, exercises to strengthen the muscles surrounding the shoulder blade are important. These muscles, the scapular stabilizers, work very hard during tennis strokes and overhead arm motions. Increasing the strength in these muscles will help to prevent shoulder injuries by providing a stable base from which the arm can work. Remember that playing tennis develops strength and endurance in the muscles in front of the body (pectorals and deltoids) but not necessarily the matching muscles in the upper back (see figure 10.4). Therefore, you should include scapular stabilizing exercises to prevent shoulder injury. As with other upper body exercises for tennis, a relatively low resistance level and high amount of repetitions are recommended to train the endurance component of these muscles due to the repetitive nature of tennis. See the page numbers in parentheses for descriptions of the following scapular stabilizing exercises:

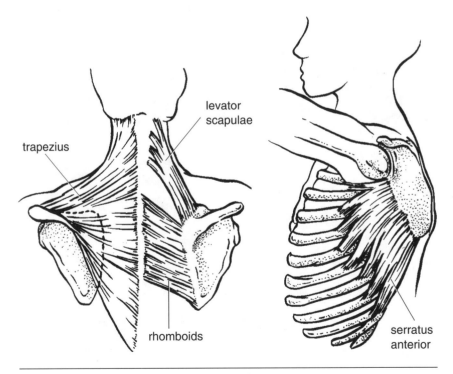

Figure 10.4   Upper back and scapular muscles.

- Seated row (p. 90)
- Bent-over row (p. 90)
- Shoulder shrug (p. 92)
- Shoulder punches (p. 93)

MODIFIED PUSH-UP

Starting Position: Begin in a standard push-up position: rest on your hands, shoulder-width apart, with your body in a straight line from the tips of your toes to the top of your head.

Note: You may need to start off on your knees if you are unable to start with a standard push-up position.

Exercise Action: Bend your elbows, lower yourself about halfway down to the floor, and then push yourself upward until your elbows are straight. At the end of the motion, round your shoulders back like a cat. Hold this position for two to three seconds. Repeat.

STEP-UP

Starting Position: Begin in a standard push-up position. Place a six-inch step on the floor next to your racket arm. (Phone books can be used and stacked to make about a six-inch step.)

Exercise Action: Place your racket arm up onto the step and then press yourself upward, rounding your shoulder and back like a "cat" while your opposite hand is placed up on the step next to your racket hand. Step back to the floor moving your non-racket hand to the floor first, followed by the racket arm and repeat.

Note: You can perform the repetitions moving toward the non-racket side if you have time.

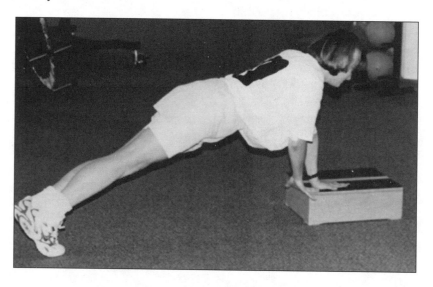

Shoulder Flexibility

Flexibility is also important in preventing shoulder injury. Research on top players has demonstrated a typical pattern of looseness and tightness in the playing shoulder. Tennis players tend to be too loose in external rotation (rotating the shoulder back, as in the cocking position of a serve), yet tight or limited in internal rotation.

Following a regimen of rotator cuff and scapular (upper back) strengthening exercise and developing your shoulder internal rotation flexibility are two important aspects of preventing shoulder injuries. Figure 10.5 illustrates a shoulder stretch that can be used to improve internal rotation flexibility. (Also see page 40 in chapter 3 for additional shoulder stretches.)

©1998 Alese and Morton Pechter

Figure 10.5   Shoulder stretch to improve internal rotation flexibility.

Using proper biomechanical stroke technique is another ingredient that you should not overlook. Consult your local tennis professional or coach to determine whether your strokes contain movement flaws that increase your potential for injury and limit your performance.

TRUNK AND LOW-BACK INJURIES

Injuries to the trunk and lower back afflict many tennis players. In a survey of 148 male professional tennis players, 38 percent reported missing a tournament due to a low-back injury. Developing power in tennis is often a function of how well the upper and lower parts of the body are connected. The trunk forms a solid unit, capable of producing great power through rotation; it also links the power generated by the lower extremities and transfers it to the arms. This transfer of forces, starting from the feet pushing against the ground; transferring up the legs through the knees, hips, and trunk; and funneled through the shoulder to the elbow, wrist, and ultimately the racket head, is termed the *kinetic link principle*.

Training the trunk muscles optimizes your ability to apply the kinetic link system in generating power for your strokes, and it is a major factor in preventing injury. A strong trunk not only prevents injuries in the lower back, but also prevents shoulder and elbow injures by providing a stable platform and force generator, taking stress off the arm.

Changes in stroke techniques in the modern game, as we outlined in chapter 1, result in a great demand on trunk rotation, particularly in the open stance forehand. A powerful open stance forehand weapon requires a huge transfer of force through the trunk, with additional power produced by segmental rotation and derotation of the trunk. The amount of trunk rotation with this open stance forehand, and with the inside-out forehand used when stepping or running around a potential backhand, is far greater than in the classic forehand. For this to safely occur, the abdominals and low-back muscles must provide support to the vertebrae, discs, and ligaments in the lower back.

Training the abdominal muscles has been stressed by sport scientists since research in the mid-1980s demonstrated high activity levels in the abdominal muscles during virtually all tennis strokes. Recent research conducted by the USTA has shown that a muscular imbalance exists in skilled junior players. Measuring abdominal and low-back strength showed the relationship between muscle groups in the skilled tennis player to be opposite that of the general population. Tennis players had greater abdominal strength and less back extension strength. This study demonstrates the importance of a balanced approach to strengthening the trunk.

To make a trunk-strengthening program specific for tennis requires exercises that match the movement patterns of the tennis player. The oblique muscles (internal and external obliques) are abdominal muscles primarily responsible for trunk rotation (see figure 3.2, a-b). They work with the rectus abdominus and back extensor muscles (erector spinae and gluteals) to support the spine. Therefore, because rotation is prevalent on every tennis stroke, strengthening exercises for the trunk typically include rotation. The following exercises use medicine balls, body weight, and machines; involve twisting and turning; and represent stresses similar to playing tennis.

Trunk-Strengthening Program

See chapter 4 for descriptions of the following trunk-strengthening exercises:

- Crunch (p. 76)
- Crossover crunch (p. 77)
- Reverse sit-up (p. 78)

- Hip raises (p. 78)
- Diagonal sit-up (p. 79)
- Sit-up with legs raised (p. 79)
- Rotary torso machine (p. 80)
- Russian twist (p. 81)
- Hip rotation (p. 81)
- Medicine ball exercises (p. 98)
- Seated trunk twists (p. 100)

Regard the trunk area as if it were a cylinder. You must address all sides of the cylinder. We recommend beginning with a program of 8 to 10 trunk exercises and increasing as your needs require. Again, use low resistance initially (body weight or four- to six-pound medicine ball), and perform an endurance number of repetitions per set, for example, 12 to 20. You can also use a time-based exercise set, performing exercises for 30 to 60 seconds per set. As your strength improves, gradually increase the amount of weight. We recommend using a high number of repetitions, because the trunk musculature is always working, even when you're not hitting the ball.

Trunk and Low-Back Flexibility

Flexibility for the trunk and hips is an important factor in preventing injury to the lower back. Of all the inflexibilities that can develop from playing tennis, tightness in the hamstrings is particularly harmful for your lower back. Hamstring tightness decreases the motion available at your hips, and it stresses your back by forcing it to move more than if the hamstrings were flexible and hips mobile.

These are the stretches from chapter 3 that are beneficial for preventing low-back injury:

- Figure 4 hamstring stretch (p. 46)
- Hamstring super stretch (p. 48)
- Hip twist (p. 53)
- Piriformis stretch (p. 54)
- Hip rotator stretch (p. 55)
- Knee to chest flex (p. 58)
- Spinal twist (seated trunk rotation) (p. 60)

Using the strength and flexibility exercises in this book will help prevent injury to the trunk and lower back. Proper mechanics are also important in preventing trunk and low-back injuries.

TENNIS ELBOW

One injury commonly associated with tennis is tennis elbow, technically called humeral epicondylitis. This term refers to the overuse injury resulting from repetitive trauma to the tendons that control wrist and forearm movement. The tendons outside your elbow raise the back of your hand toward you (extension) and are the most commonly involved tendons in tennis elbow. This is lateral (outside) tennis elbow and usually results from improper technique during backhands. However, it can be caused by any tennis stroke because these muscles and tendons undergo stress during all tennis movements with the arm.

Medial, or inside, tennis elbow involves the tendons that bend your wrist down (flexion) and cause rotation (pronation) of your forearm. This form of tennis elbow is more common among highly skilled tennis players, baseball pitchers, and golfers. These muscles and tendons are stressed the most during the forehand, the serve, and techniques that do not involve power from the legs and trunk. Instead they use the elbow, wrist, and hand to produce power, placing the player at risk of developing this injury.

The good news about tennis elbow is that, in 90 percent of cases, surgery is not required to get rid of it, and it is preventable. How do you prevent tennis elbow? The single biggest factor in preventing tennis elbow is using proper biomechanical tennis stroke technique. As mentioned previously, strokes that use the muscles in the forearm and wrist to generate power are particularly stressful to tendons in the elbow. A leading elbow backhand is a classic example of an improper stroke technique that can cause lateral tennis elbow. Strokes using a "wristy" technique are also bad. We recommend that you consult your tennis professional to have your strokes evaluated *before* you have an injury.

Elbow Strength

Strengthening exercises involve a light weight (starting with as little as two to five pounds), using 30 to 45 repetitions of movement patterns that emphasize the wrist and forearm. Make sure you consult a physician or physical therapist if you are rehabilitating an elbow injury. In chapter 4, page 90 we recommend exercises that you can perform to improve strength and muscular endurance. Take care to isolate the movements at the wrist and hand, and do not use the upper body or trunk to cheat. You can also use rubber tubing effectively to strengthen these muscles. Adding the following rubber tubing exercises to your strengthening program will help prevent tennis elbow and optimize your performance.

WRIST CURLS—EXTENSORS

Starting Position: Stabilize the forearm palm down on your thigh. Place one end of the surgical tubing under your foot and grasp the other end with your hand.

Exercise Action: Begin with your wrist bent down. Slowly raise your hand, keeping your forearm on your thigh. Hold for a count; then slowly return to the starting position. All movement should occur at the wrist, not the elbow. Repeat.

WRIST CURLS—FLEXORS

Starting Position: Stabilize your forearm palm up on your thigh. Place one end of the surgical tubing under your foot and grasp the other end with your hand.

Exercise Action: Begin with the wrist bent down. Slowly raise your hand, keeping your forearm on your thigh. Hold for a count; then slowly return to the starting position. All movement should occur at the wrist, not the elbow. Repeat.

RADIAL CURLS

Starting Position: Stabilize your forearm on your thigh in a neutral or thumb up position. Place one end of the tubing under your foot and grasp the other end in your hand.

Exercise Action: Begin with your wrist bent down; then flex it upward. Hold for a count and slowly return to starting position. All movement should occur at the wrist. You will not be able to exercise through a large arc of movement. Repeat.

Elbow Flexibility

Flexibility is an important part of preventing tennis elbow. See chapter 3, page 40 for stretches that directly address the elbow, forearm, and wrist. Tennis players need these stretches because both junior and senior tennis players lose the ability to completely straighten (extend) their elbows on their dominant (racket) side. Perform these stretches before and after tennis play. Remember to hold each stretch for about 15 to 20 seconds.

WRIST INJURIES

It's not often that doing one thing gives you the bonus of accomplishing two things at once! However, the exercise program for tennis elbow appears to do just that. The same strengthening and flexibility exercises you would do for preventing tennis elbow also prevent wrist injuries. Changes in the game, including stiffer or longer rackets, more powerful strokes, and the prevalence of fast, hard courts, can increase stress to the wrist. Several top players in the last few years have had serious wrist injuries that resulted in time away from the game.

Increasing strength and endurance of the muscles that cross the wrist helps to protect the wrist and the ligaments that keep the wrist together. In addition to strength and flexibility exercises, proper technique and selecting equipment appropriate for your style and body play a critical role.

ARM INJURIES

Several aspects of your tennis equipment can affect your arm. String tension is one important factor. The tighter your strings are the more control you will have; the looser the strings the more powerful your racket becomes. We recommend decreasing your string tension a few pounds (two to four) when you are having shoulder, elbow, or wrist pain. Lower string tension reduces impact shock and increases the power of your racket slightly, so you don't have to work as hard. Decreasing the tension too much, however, will lead to a loss of control and possible damaging consequences, as you may change your stroke technique to accommodate this increased power.

Vibration dampeners have no affect on your arm. Research performed by noted physicist Dr. Howard Brody has shown that these dampeners do affect high-frequency vibration, such as that coming off your strings. That explains the change in sound when playing with a vibration dampeners. The high-frequency vibration does not affect your arm, however. Dr. Brody points out that these objects do not absorb low-frequency vibration from the racket, which is the type that damages your arm. Although these devices do not hurt your arm, they technically will not help your arm.

Racket stiffness is another factor to think about if you have an arm injury. Sports medicine professionals and scientists recommend rackets that are of midrange stiffness. Playing with a racket that is too stiff will cause more abrupt shock or jarring sensations to the arm, compared with a more flexible racket.

Following the manufacturer's guidelines for racket string tension and looking for a medium stiff frame will assist you in choosing equipment that is right for your arm. Consult your certified tennis professional or racket technician (stringer) for further guidance. Don't change your equipment just before big tournaments or periods of heavy tennis play. This will allow you to get used to your new or changed equipment gradually. Changes in equipment or technique are the two most common causes of tennis-related injuries.

KNEE INJURIES

One final area of prevention we will discuss here is injuries to the knee joint. Tennis obviously places a great deal of stress on the knee joints from bending, quick starts and stops, and explosive accelerations. Because tennis is a noncontact sport, the bone-crushing knee injuries we equate with football or skiing are not prevalent. Instead, injures to the kneecap (patello-femoral joint) are probably the most disabling among tennis players. The kneecap, or patella as it is technically termed, rides in a shallow groove at the end of your thigh bone, or femur.

With repeated stress to the legs, such as tennis play, and without sufficient strength and endurance of the thigh muscles (especially the quadriceps), the kneecap can become irritated. This irritation is caused by lack of support from the surrounding muscles as you fatigue, which prevents the kneecap from gliding freely in the groove at the end of the thigh bone. This repeated irritation can wear down the back side of the kneecap and produce significant pain. You can wear braces to support the kneecap, but ultimately support should come from the muscles.

Preventing knee injuries in tennis focuses on two strategies: strength and flexibility. To strengthen your knees, use the appropriate exercises described in chapter 4. One additional consideration is critical when performing knee exercises. It involves using a limited movement pattern to decrease the stress to the knees during exercise.

Pressure between the kneecap and the end of the femur, or thigh bone, is greatest when the knee is bent between 45 and 60 degrees while doing a leg extension type exercise pictured in chapter 4, page 72. Because this is the part of the movement that is particularly stressful, individuals who are having knee pain and players with a history of knee injury should avoid it. It is also necessary for those players with achy knees to avoid deep squats, lunges, or leg press movements in which the knees bend more than 90 degrees. These exercises cause great stress while the muscles are being strengthened. Following are strength exercises and stretches that will prevent injury to your knees.

Strength Exercises to Prevent Knee Injury

See chapter 4 for descriptions of the following exercises:

- Leg press (p. 72)
- Leg extension (partial range if indicated) (p. 72)
- Multi-hip (p. 73)
- Hamstring curl (p. 73)
- Partial squat (p. 74)
- Lunges (multidirectional) (p. 74)
- Leg raises with cuff weights (p. 75)

Stretches to Prevent Knee Injury

See chapter 3 for descriptions of the following stretches:

- Figure 4 hamstring stretch (p. 46)
- Hamstring super stretch (p. 48)
- Stork quadriceps stretch (p. 49)
- Prone quadriceps stretch (p. 50)
- Hip rotator stretch (p. 55)
- Iliotibial band stretch (p. 56)

Tennis players can follow these important strategies to prevent injury in these commonly stressed areas. Using both strength and flexibility exercises, with proper biomechanics, forms the platform for an injury-prevention program.

BIOMECHANICS

A repeating theme among the prevention strategies for common tennis injuries is using proper biomechanics. We cannot stress this enough. Each injury in this chapter can be caused by improper and inefficient stroke mechanics. Knowing how the kinetic link principle applies to hitting a tennis ball will show you how important proper stroke mechanics can be.

Tennis strokes that just use the shoulder, elbow, and wrist to generate power will result in injury. Throughout this book, we have described conditioning programs that emphasize leg, trunk, and shoulder strength. These are the primary muscles involved in generating power and, with proper training, will prevent tennis injuries. To ensure that your tennis strokes involve efficient movement patterns, consider these recommendations:

- Consult your tennis professional for a technique lesson.
- Consult your tennis professional again if you change your mechanics or notice difficulties with a stroke.
- Use a video camcorder, if available, so you and your teaching professional can study your movement and stroke mechanics.

PREVENTING HEAT ILLNESS

Another area we will discuss in this chapter is preventing heat illness. Although not a musculoskeletal injury, heat stress is a common ailment with tennis play. It can include heat cramps, heat exhaustion, and most seriously, heat stroke. The most widely recommended prevention strategies for heat illness are proper fluid hydration and nutritional intake.

While playing tennis in the heat, the body's primary cooling mechanism comes from sweating. Sweat rates in male and female tennis players can range between 0.5 and 2.5 liters per hour, depending on fitness level, environmental temperature, and hydration status. In addition to water, electrolytes are also lost in sweat. Sodium and chloride are the primary electrolytes lost during sweating, with potassium and magnesium also lost. Contrary to popular belief, sport scientists now suggest that sodium loss with heavy sweating may be the largest causative factor in heat cramps.

Thirst is not an adequate stimulus for hydration, because a player can lose as much as 1.5 liters of water before perceiving thirst. Therefore, proper hydration involves drinking before you are thirsty and hydrating before tennis play. Drinking fluids the night before and early in the day before tennis play improves a player's prematch hydration status. While playing, drink during every changeover, even if you are not thirsty. Remember, the thirst mechanism is not a reliable indicator of fluid need.

© Russ Adams Productions, Inc.

Hydrate using water or a suitable fluid replacement beverage that has electrolytes you lose during heavy sweating. Always use a fluid replacement beverage that you have tried in practice. Never try a new one for the first time during a match.

During periods of heavy sweat loss, replacing sodium becomes important. We do not recommend salt pills; they irritate the stomach and intestine. Therefore, salt foods more heavily, and use an electrolyte replacement beverage that you have tested to replace electrolytes along with water. Whenever possible, acclimate yourself to the area you will be playing in before competition. It takes 7 to 10 days to fully acclimate to a new climate. Benefits of acclimation include better sweat rates, sweating earlier in response to heat stress, and less sodium loss at the sweat gland.

Hydration Tips for Tennis

Drink cool water or sport drinks during play. Sport drinks are especially helpful during long matches, in hot weather, and for recovery after play. Use a similar routine (as described below) before, during, and after practice.

Before Play:
- Drink fluids often throughout the day.
- Drink 12-16 ounces about an hour before play begins.
- Prepare at least two quarts (64 ounces) to drink during play; sport drinks are preferable for long matches or during play in hot weather.

During Play:
- Drink four to eight ounces (four to eight normal swallows) after the warm-up and during every changeover.

After Play:
- Immediately begin to replace fluid, electrolytes, and carbohydrates with water, sport drinks, and food; high carbohydrate sport drinks are very effective if you are going to play again soon.
- Drink at least a pint (16 ounces) of fluid for every pound of body weight deficit.
- Consider adding salt to your food and/or drinks if sweat losses were extensive.

Following a total conditioning program for tennis provides what you need to prevent injury and optimize performance. Your knowledge of the information in this chapter will give you the strategies to prevent heat illness through proper hydration and minimize your chances of common musculoskeletal injuries.

ABOUT THE AUTHOR

The **United States Tennis Association (USTA)** is the governing body for tennis in the United States. The USTA's membership consists of more than 500,000 individuals and nearly 6,500 organizations, including schools, park and recreation departments or community tennis associations, and tennis clubs.

The USTA is widely known as the owner and operator of the U.S. Open Championships, one of the four Grand Slam tournaments in worldwide tennis competition. The U.S. Open annually attracts more than a half-million fans, awards more than $9 million in prize money, and is broadcast on television to 125 countries.

The USTA also sponsors amateur tennis competition for players of all ages and abilities, ranging from events for children 12 and under to national tournaments for those 65 and older. More than 5 million schoolchildren are introduced to tennis each year through USTA school programs, and opportunities for further instruction and play are provided by a menu of USTA entry-level programs.

A full range of player development, sport science, and youth tennis programs is offered at the USTA training facility in Key Biscayne, FL, at 120 Area Training Centers spread throughout the country, and through local Excellence Training Programs. In addition, the USTA emphasizes coaching education and development through an ambitious offering of coaching seminars, workshops, and conferences.

The USTA developed *Complete Conditioning for Tennis* with the help of Paul Roetert and Todd Ellenbecker. **Paul Roetert** is the USTA Sport Science Administrator in Key Biscayne, FL. Roetert received his PhD in biomechanics at the University of Connecticut and is a Fellow in the American College of Sports Medicine. Roetert is a certified tennis teaching professional with the United States Professional Tennis Association (USPTA) and United States Professional Tennis Registry (USPTR). **Todd Ellenbecker** is a physical therapist and clinic director of Physiotherapy Associates Scottsdale Sports Clinic in Scottsdale, AZ. He received his therapy degree from the University of Wisconsin-LaCrosse and a master's degree in exercise physiology from Arizona State University. In addition, he is a certified sports clinical specialist by the American Physical Therapy Association (APTA), and a certified strength and conditioning specialist.

MORE TENNIS TITLES FROM HK

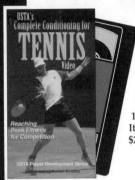

This action-packed video presents a functional training program, showing proper technique for essential tennis conditioning exercises, the connection between the exercises in the drills and better performance on the tennis court, and a training schedule so players peak for key competitions.

1997 • 25-minute videotape
Item MUST0918 • ISBN 0-88011-918-7
$24.95 ($37.50 Canadian)

Tennis Tactics presents 58 strategic shot sequences to maximize your strengths and exploit your opponents' weaknesses. Includes 63 drills that show you how to practice the shot patterns and make them part of your tactical approach in match play.

Winning Patterns of Play features actual U.S. Open footage of professional tennis players using their favorite strategies and showing you how to execute backcourt, midcourt, net play, and defensive patterns; perform practice drills that will give you the edge in competition; choose patterns that emphasize your strengths; and recognize, anticipate, and react to your opponents' patterns.

Book • 1996 • Paper • 248 pp • Item PUST0499
ISBN 0-88011-499-1 • $14.95 ($20.95 Canadian)

Video • 1995 • 20-minute videotape
Item MUST0464 • $17.95 ($26.95 Canadian)

Special Book and Video Package
1/2" VHS and *Tennis Tactics* book
Item MUST0473 • $29.95 ($44.95 Canadian)

Prices subject to change.

For more information or to place your order,
U.S. customers call toll-free **1-800-747-4457**. Customers outside the U.S. use the appropriate telephone number/address shown in the front of this book.

HUMAN KINETICS
The Premier Publisher for Sports & Fitness
www.humankinetics.com

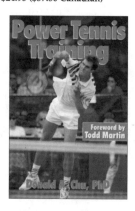